A NEW MAP

RICA,

...IA ISLANDS.

DIVIDED

according to the Preliminary Articles of
Peace, Signed at Versailles, 20. Jan. 1783.

wherein are particularly Distinguished

THE UNITED STATES,

and the *SEVERAL PROVINCES, GOVERNMENTS* &c.
which Compose

THE BRITISH DOMINIONS,

Laid down according to THE LATEST SURVEYS,
and Corrected *from* THE ORIGINAL MATERIALS,
of Gover. POWNALL, Mem. of Parlia.

1783.

Officially Indian

OFFICIALLY
INDIAN

Symbols That Define
the United States

Cécile R. Ganteaume

Foreword by Colin G. Calloway
Afterword by Paul Chaat Smith

Published by the
NATIONAL MUSEUM OF THE AMERICAN INDIAN

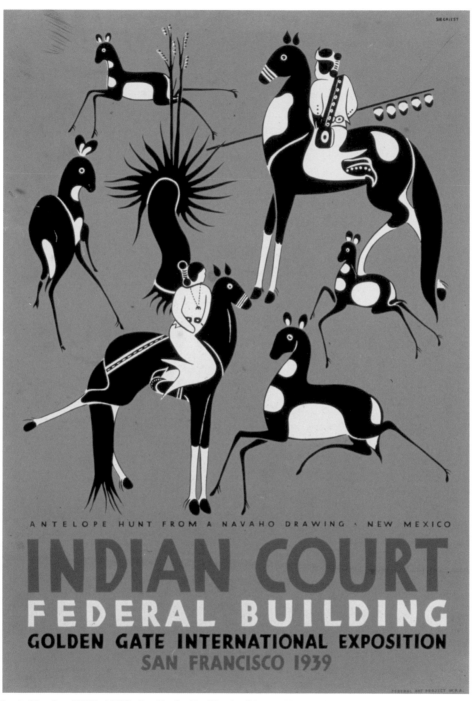

Louis Siegriest (1899–1985) after Ha-So-De (Narciso Platero Abeyta [Diné], 1918–1998). Golden Gate International Exposition poster, 1939. Silkscreened print. Courtesy of the Library of Congress Prints and Photographs Division, WPA Poster Collection

The National Museum of the American Indian (NMAI), Smithsonian Institution, is committed to advancing knowledge and understanding of the Native cultures of the Western Hemisphere—past, present, and future—through partnership with Native people and others. The museum works to support the continuance of culture, traditional values, and transitions in contemporary Native life.

For more information about the Smithsonian's National Museum of the American Indian, visit its website at www.AmericanIndian.si.edu. To support the museum by becoming a member, call 1-800-242-NMAI (6624) or click "Support" on the website.

Director: Kevin Gover (Pawnee)

Associate Director for Museum Research and Scholarship: David W. Penney

Publications Manager: Tanya Thrasher (Cherokee Nation)

Assistant Publications Manager: Ann Kawasaki

Project Editor: Sally Barrows

Design: Steve Bell

Editorial and Research Assistance: Christine T. Gordon, Julie B. Macander, Jane McAllister, Alexandra Harris Schupman (Cherokee), Vector Talent Resources

Rights and Permissions: Wendy Hurlock Baker, Julie B. Macander

Index: Kate Mertes

Published in conjunction with the exhibition *Americans*, opening at the National Museum of the American Indian in Washington, DC, in October 2017.

First Edition

10 9 8 7 6 5 4 3 2 1

Printed in Canada

Library of Congress Cataloging-in-Publication Data

Names: Ganteaume, Cécile R., author.

Title: Officially Indian : symbols that define the United States / by Cécile R. Ganteaume.

Description: First edition. | Washington, DC : Smithsonian Institution, National Museum of the American Indian, 2017. | "Published in conjunction with the exhibition Americans, opening at the National Museum of the American Indian, Washington, D.C. on October 26, 2017." Includes bibliographical references and index.

Identifiers: LCCN 2017013825 (print) | LCCN 2017023018 (ebook) | ISBN 978-1-4529-5688-6 (e-book) | ISBN 978-1-5179-0330-5 (hardcover : alkaline paper)

Subjects: LCSH: Indians of North America—Pictorial works—Exhibitions. | Indians in art—Exhibitions. | Signs and symbols—United States—Exhibitions. | Signs and symbols—Political aspects—United States—History—Exhibitions. | National characteristics, American—History—Exhibitions. | Nationalism—United States—History—Exhibitions. | United States—Race relations—Political aspects—History—Exhibitions. National Museum of the American Indian (Washington, D.C.)—Exhibitions.

Classification: LCC E77.5 (ebook) | LCC E77.5 .G37 2017 (print) | DDC 970.004/97—dc23

LC record available at https://lccn.loc.gov/2017013825

Cover: Indian-head nickel, 1913; minted 1935. James Earle Fraser (1876–1953), designer. Stamped copper and nickel. Courtesy of the Numismatic Guaranty Corporation, Sarasota, Florida.

Frontispiece: White Mountain Apache tribal chairman Ronnie Lupe (right) gives the traditional Apache sacred blessing to the first Apache Block III aircraft, 2011. With him (left) is Ramon Riley (detail). Photo by Sofia Bledsoe. Courtesy of Defense Video Imagery Distribution System. The full version of this photo appears on page 147.

Distributed by the University of Minnesota Press

111 Third Avenue South, Suite 290

Minneapolis, MN 55401-2520

www.upress.umn.edu

Table of Contents

FOREWORD

COLIN G. CALLOWAY

EARLY IN JUNE 1781, Jean Baptiste Ducoigne and a delegation of Kaskaskia Indians who had traveled from the Illinois country visited Thomas Jefferson, just as his term as governor of Virginia was ending. Jefferson told them: "We, like you, are Americans, born in the same land, and having the same interests" (Boyd et al. 1952, 60). It was a curious statement from the man who five years earlier in the Declaration of Independence had demonized Indians as the savage pawns of a tyrannical English king, bloodthirsty warriors unleashed on the American frontier to murder innocent people without regard for age or gender. But the Revolutionary War was still raging and Jefferson was not the only rebel leader to make such a statement to Indian nations, which still had power to influence its outcome. From the moment the Revolution broke out, the Americans and British had competed for their allegiance. The British pointed to their policies of conducting relations by treaty and affording some protection to Indian lands, which compared favorably in Native eyes with the aggressive land hunger of the "Big Knives." Jefferson and others countered by invoking a shared history and identity with Indians: colonial Americans and Native Americans lived on this continent and belonged here; the British did not.

Jefferson's declaration that Indians and Americans were citizens of the same land was surely no more than a moment of wartime expediency, or another instance of the hypocrisy and duplicity of which the third president so often has been accused. Americans had no interest in sharing their identity with Indians, and they had no interest in sharing the land, either. The United States at the end of the Revolution had won its independence, but it was a long way from being a nation, and it had precious few resources with which to build one. What it did have was vast amounts of land, or at least a claim to all the territory south of Canada, north of Florida, and east of the Mississippi River that Britain had transferred to it at the Peace of Paris in 1783. With an empty treasury and little to unite individual states, the new nation looked to western lands to furnish revenue for the government, profits for speculators, and homes for citizens. The infant United States would not likely survive penned in east of the Appalachians; its future depended on expanding west to the Mississippi. But that land belonged to Indian peoples, who saw no reason to give it up because a distant king who never owned it had given it to someone else. Any fellow feeling Americans had towards Indians, even those who had fought alongside them during the Revolution, quickly dissipated as the expanding republic proceeded to dispossess them and drive them from the country. By war and treaty, coercion and deception, Americans built a nation on Indian lands. They also built a sense of identity and nationhood in the shared experience of overcoming Indian resistance, a process they called winning the West.

From its earliest days, the United States justified its expropriation of Indian land by offering the blessings of civilization to people it portrayed as savages. In reality, the two elements worked hand in hand. Indians were told they could survive in the modern world only if they became "civilized." That meant Indian men must give up hunting and take up farming. "Surplus" hunting territory could then be sold to white farmers. Turning Indians into property-owning, American-style farmers was consistent with a broader U.S. Indian policy predicated on the seizure of tribal homelands. But the process was slow, and the young republic was impatient. In 1830 Congress passed the Indian Removal Act, making national policy the relocation of thousands of Indian people—even those deemed civilized—from the eastern United States to territories on the other side of the Mississippi. In the West, as the United States drove to the Pacific under the banner of manifest destiny and reuniting the nation after the Civil War, it confined Indians to reservations, where they would be out of the way and could be subjected to intensive policies of assimilation. By 1887 Indian landholdings in the United States had shrunk to less than 140 million acres. The Dawes Allotment Act, passed through Congress that year, aimed to accelerate the civilization process by breaking up communally held reservation lands and allotting them in 160-acre parcels of individually owned property. By the time the act was repealed in 1934, Indian landholdings had diminished by an additional 90 million acres. The attack on tribal homelands was part of a sustained war on tribal ways of life, waged against children in boarding schools far from home as well as against the moral economy and traditions of Indian communities.

Having developed and implemented policies and practices to deprive Indian peoples of their lands and destroy their cultures, Americans proceeded to construct a history of the United States that ignored the Indians' past and denied their presence. Jean Baptiste Ducoigne named his son Thomas Jefferson, but Jefferson's words rang hollow: Americans might claim to share the continent with the indigenous inhabitants, but what they really wanted was their absence. Nevertheless,

Americans who employed and created images of Indians as savages to justify their dispossession also employed and created images of Indians to understand themselves and used their ideas about Indians to shape national identity. How they viewed themselves changed how they viewed Indians (Berkhofer, Jr 1978).

By the end of the nineteenth century, the Native American population reached its nadir: just 237,000, according to the U.S. census of 1900. But Indians haunted the American memory and persisted in the national story as historical curiosities (Bergland 2000). Americans now created romantic images about the people they had defeated and dispossessed, and the stereotype of the savage warrior gave way to the stereotype of the disappearing Indian. James Earl Fraser's iconic sculpture, *The End of the Trail*, depicting a weary Indian warrior slumped over his dying pony, reflected American sentiments about the destiny of the first Americans. In the photographs of Edward Curtis, and in the imaginations of many Americans, "real" Indians faded into the sunset, disappeared from American history, and were replaced by abstract and idealized Natives acting out prescribed roles (Gidley 1998).

Meanwhile, Americans faced or imagined threats from elsewhere, as millions of immigrants arrived in the United States from southern and eastern Europe. "Older" Americans, who traced their descent from northern and western Europe, feared the foreign-born newcomers would dilute the American character and erode the values that had built the nation. Confronted by a rising tide of immigrants who needed to be Americanized, Anglo Americans turned to Native Americans who seemed to be disappearing to help them define themselves. They began to find, create, and invoke images of Indian people, history, and culture to represent and reassert what they imagined to be the best of their own characteristics, history, and culture. Indians, like other real Americans, stood for freedom, courage, pride, patriotism, and the values of an earlier era. Images of Indian "primitivism" and Indian warriors were appropriated to represent distinctly American traits. Once obstacles to American nation building, they could now be symbols of American national identity (Trachtenberg 2004). As during the Revolution, Americans identified with Indians as native-born inhabitants of the continent.

At the same time, writers who were drawn to Indian societies as alternatives to urban and industrial America found much to admire, and they helped change popular images and ideas about Indians from negative to positive (Smith 2000). Non-Indians "playing Indian"—appropriating Indian dress and acting out Indian roles for a variety of reasons—has a long history, stretching back to the Boston Tea Party and beyond, and now businesses, clubs, scouting organizations, schools, colleges, and sports teams latched on to stereotypical images of Indians as warriors, athletes, and children of nature. They adopted what they thought to be Indian names, words, symbols, motifs, rituals, and dress to display their membership, express their "spirit," and represent identities that were "unquestionably American" (Deloria 1998, 183).

Modern-day Americans continue to appropriate aspects of Indian cultures to sell their products or claim connections with a way of life that appears more spiritual and more moral than the one they experience in the dominant capitalist society. Indian logos advertised and helped sell tobacco in the eighteenth century and still do. Americans buy butter in packets adorned with an Indian maiden and drive automobiles named after Indian tribes and chiefs. Sports teams employ Indian mascots, sometimes citing approval from Indian people, often in defiance of Indian protest. At best, such practices of cultural cooption may be little more than harmless examples in a long tradition of playing Indian; at worst, and all too often, they present vicious caricatures, perpetuate dangerous racial and sexual stereotypes, and have negative psychological impacts that have been well documented.[1] Ongoing conflicts—and lawsuits—about representations of American Indians in popular culture reflect enduring uncertainties and tensions about the place of Native people in American society.

This book looks beyond images of Indians in popular culture. From the earliest days of the republic, the United States *government* has also employed representations of Indian people and Indian-ness as emblems of national identity. Images of Indians appear in official publications and on maps; on seals and certificates; on stamps, medals, and coins; on and in public buildings; on monuments and bridges. Warplanes, helicopters, and missiles bear Indian names and logos; military insignia incorporate Indian symbols. Indians featured in national events—five chiefs, including the notorious Apache, Geronimo, rode in Theodore Roosevelt's inaugural parade in 1905. Presidents and presidential candidates have been photographed wearing Plains Indian–style feather headdresses. Patriotic societies likewise have employed images of Indians as expressions of their identity and love of country. Like Jefferson's words to Ducoigne, such attempts to depict Indians as part of a shared American past, a national identity, or a common cause may appear hypocritical, laughable, and cynical when viewed against the troubled history and harsh realities of Indian relations in this country.

Yet examining the official use of Indian images, explaining its purposes, and exploring its different meanings for different people at different times tells us much about the United States and how it sees or wants to see itself. Why would a country that devoted so much of its history to removing Indian people choose Indians to represent itself? Why would a nation whose founding document identified Indians as allies of tyranny deploy images of Indians to stand for American democracy? Why would the most powerful government in the world identify with people who suffered and survived its power? Why would a nation that confined its indigenous people and denied their rights present Indians to the world as symbols of American freedom?

To address such questions, Cécile Ganteaume provides context and interpretation for nearly fifty representations and national emblems, ranging from the earliest European woodcuts to the series of U. S. congressional gold medals struck in 2013 in formal if belated recognition of the thirty-three Indian nations that provided code talkers for the U.S. armed forces in two world wars. Each description and discussion stands in its own right as a study of a particular image, emblem, sculpture, photograph, or event. Taken together, they form a gallery of America's fascination with American Indians and the multiple dimensions of what has been called the white man's Indian.

Americans did not invent the practice of using American Indians as expressions of American identity; they inherited it. From as early as the sixteenth century, Europeans depicted America as an Indian, often a woman, usually wearing an upright feather headdress, a plumed skirt of feathers, and not much else. Indian figures commonly adorned maps of the "New World." Despite the fact that Europeans in America often defined themselves in opposition to the Indians with whom they contested the continent, the colonists, too, began to depict America as an Indian, who now stood as well for freedom from British imperial rule. The protesters who dressed like Indians to dump tea into Boston Harbor employed a language of symbolism their intended audience would have understood.

Although most Indians who fought in the Revolution sided with the British, and indigenous wars of independence from American domination continued for years to come, the new government continued to employ images of Indians to represent America, which now meant the United States, a nation without yet a clear sense of nationhood. As the United States took its place on the world stage, it faced west to Indian nations as well as east to the nations of Europe. Facing west, it built an empire on Indian land; facing east, it distinguished itself from the other nations by using Indian emblems. Indians and their associated symbols now represented what the Founding Fathers and the revolutionary generation had fought for: liberty and democracy. Designs for the Great Seal of the United States included an Indian figure. U.S. congressional medals presented to Revolutionary War heroes and a diplomatic medal, conceived by Jefferson and approved by George Washington as a gift to departing foreign dignitaries, employed an Indian Queen to represent the United States. Ironically, as the United States used Indian figures to represent itself as a nation committed to freedom, it embarked on a path of expansion and colonialism that deprived Indian people of their freedom and denied them a place in American society.

In response, Indian people waged sustained resistance, not simply against American occupation of their lands, but also against continuing assaults on their lives and languages, resources and rights, families and future. The association of Indians with freedom that became entrenched and endured in American imagination and imagery stemmed in large part from the Indians' fight for freedom *against* the United States, a struggle that was seen as heroic yet tragically and inevitably futile. Indians were both emblems of freedom and, as in many of the paintings that subsequently adorned public buildings, symbols of a vanishing race.

American Indians, of course, did not vanish. They survived American colonialism and caricatures, and they may outlast the United States itself. Almost two and a half centuries since it first depicted itself as an American Indian, the United States is still figuring out its relationships, and sometimes its attitudes, toward American Indians and the nearly 570 Native nations with which it shares its territory. That the United States has so often and in so many ways employed images of American Indians to depict itself gives lie to assumptions and assertions that Indians did not matter in the history of this nation. They appear, in some profound way, to have been fundamental to it. The images in this book tell us little about American Indians, but they tell us a great deal about America in search of itself.

The World's Oldest Enduring Republic

CÉCILE R. GANTEAUME

FROM THE DAYS OF GEORGE WASHINGTON and Thomas Jefferson, many who have thought deeply about the United States and its foundational ideas have observed that the country is at its core a democratic experiment. In a 2015 interview, Supreme Court Justice Stephen Breyer elaborated on this view, explaining that the United States throughout its history has been dealing with the issue of what we today call human rights—the question of who may share in the benefits of democracy.[1] The question is not unique to the United States. Many of Europe's increasingly multicultural countries, for example, also are confronting it. Whether owing to warfare, famine, poverty, or international agreements, national borders are becoming more porous and populations are shifting. More people live and work in societies that are different in ethnicity, language, and religion from those into which they were born. For a democratic country that seeks to uphold ideals of liberty and equality, issues of accommodation and political integration can pose complex problems, especially when that country believes itself to be confronting such concerns for the first time in its history.

The United States is the world's oldest enduring republic devoted to the principles of liberty and equality. But its Founding Fathers and their descendants carved the republic out of indigenous lands. Generation after generation, Americans have needed to define anew their relationship with American Indians, the peoples whose lands they usurped and whom they long regarded as fundamentally different from themselves. Americans have always acknowledged that American Indians are embedded in the American experience and that the relationship with American Indians is an integral part of their heritage. In this book, however, I intend to show that from the beginning American Indians have been crucial to the United States' core identity as a democratic nation and to the ongoing national debate over what it means to be an American. I will do so by examining the United States' extraordinary habit throughout its history of using imagery of American Indians in its visual expressions of national identity, both to distinguish itself from other nations and define itself for its citizens. These visual expressions are not empty symbols. They have meaning. They represent what the country stands for. Seen collectively and studied in detail, American Indian imagery in the United States' official and semiofficial emblems sheds light on the United States' evolving sense of itself as a democratic nation.

By official emblems of national identity, I mean those created or displayed under the aegis of a wide range of U.S. government departments and agencies. These entities include the Architect of the U.S. Capitol; the Bureau of Engraving and Printing; the (former) Continental Congress; the Departments of State, Interior, and Treasury; the House of Representatives; the Indian Arts & Crafts Board; the Library of Congress; the (former) Office of the Supervising Architect; the U.S. Army, Courts, Marine Corps, Mint, Postal Service, and Senate; the White House; and the (former) Works Progress Administration (WPA).

By semiofficial emblems, I mean widely disseminated photographs of news-making national events. In the twentieth century, the twin notions of documentary photography and photojournalism gained currency, and photographs of news-making events were circulated widely. Photo-documented events in this book include inaugural parades, presidential campaigns, and even goodwill visits. Other semiofficial emblems were produced by patriotic societies. These societies include the Sons of Liberty and the Tammany Society, whose founding members had impeccable American Revolutionary War credentials; the Ladies of Powhatan County, Virginia, which was active during the American Civil War; and the Improved Order of Red Men, which was chartered by Congress and counted among its members three U.S. presidents. Considered together these emblems reveal, first, that the United States' national identity is tied inextricably to American Indians and, second, how deep, intellectually as well as temporally the roots of American Indian imagery are in expressions of that identity.

Of the scholars who have examined specific instances of the American Indian imagery employed in U.S. expressions of national identity, several have focused on the use of the Indian Princess and Indian Queen motifs and have demonstrated how colonial patriots and the first generation of Americans appropriated this politically charged imagery from the British, transforming it into a uniquely American symbol of independence and liberty (Fleming 1965, 1967; Fisher 2005; Olson 1991). Other scholars have examined artworks that were commissioned for display in the U.S. Capitol. They have analyzed those paintings and sculptures in terms of expressions of race, progress, and empire (Fryd 2001; Kennon and Somma 2004). More recently, scholars have been interested in images of American Indians created by American Indians under the aegis of President Franklin D. Roosevelt's ambitious New Deal program, the WPA (McLerran 2009). Specifically, they have examined murals in federal buildings as "premodern" representations, which they ultimately attribute to the government's inability to recognize Native modernity (ibid., 1). Very different, though related and highly germane to my analysis in this book, are studies that have examined American perceptions or rather, misperceptions of American Indians (Pearce [1953] 1967; Berkhofer Jr. 1978; Deloria 1998; Huhndorf 2001; Smith 2009). These works examine the fundamental misunderstandings that Americans continue to hold about American Indians. They also show just how deeply American Indians have seeped into Americans' cultural imaginations, by exploring the myriad ways that Americans throughout U.S. history have appropriated Native cultural identities and, in doing so, have created imaginary Indians.

Scholars have overlooked, however, the U.S. government's consistent use of American Indian imagery in its emblems of national identity. In this study, I concentrate on these emblems rather than representations of American Indians in popular culture because I am specifically concerned with how the U.S. government has understood the relationship between democracy and American Indians. The depictions discussed in this book represent a sustained conversation the country has been having with itself about American Indians and the idea of liberty and equality for all.

In the following pages, I examine the particular meanings embedded in the imagery produced by not only Americans but also Europeans, who identified the "New World" with American Indians long before the United States existed. The imagery appears in a remarkably broad range of places and spans five centuries, from the early 1500s to the present. It is found on map cartouches; tobacco advertisements; political broadsides; presidential peace medals; diplomatic medals; coins and stamps; federally commissioned paintings, sculptures, murals, and other artworks in federal buildings; Confederate flags; monuments in national cemeteries; White House decorative arts; architectural reliefs; widely disseminated photographs of national events; military weapons and insignia; and the earliest and most recent congressional gold medals. The selection of images in this book is by no means exhaustive, but it is comprehensive in that it represents a range of instances of deeply charged imagery of American Indians employed by the U.S. government and its colonial predecessors.

• • • •

In considering the U.S. government's use of American Indian imagery, one must keep in mind the obvious: American Indians were never simply a convenient foil against which the United States could define itself or at least give some sharpness to its sense of itself. Nor were they ever simply a blank slate upon which the United

States could inscribe meanings without consequences. An image is a representation, not a thing itself. Moreover, symbols are used in the real world, where conflicts and struggles take place. Academics have increasingly begun to examine the complicated relationship between Americans and American Indians in terms of settler colonialism (Wolfe 2006; Jacobs 2011; Hixson 2013; Smithers 2014; Mamdani 2015). Scholars have applied the term "settler colonialism" to the United States, especially to the country in the nineteenth century, to refer to the flagrant dispossession of American Indians of their lands; the state-sanctioned influx of European and American settlers; and the acts of aggression, violence, and human suffering that accompanied this dispossession and settlement. The term also describes the exploitation of indigenous lands for natural resources, and the lingering effects of colonialism (i.e., trauma). Inarguably, American Indians have paid a high price for Americans' belief in territorial expansionism and desire for economic, military, and political dominance. The United States had the power to expand its reach across the continent, and it did. Using settler colonialism as an analytical tool, the scholar Mahmood Mamdani has referred to the United States as not only "the world's first settler colony" but also "the place where settler colonialism triumphed" (Mamdani 2015, 613).

Yet from its founding, the United States has believed continuously that democracy is its natural destiny. And, in fact, American Indians have always been dynamic actors in the history of both Native North America and the United States of America. They have acted on their own political ambitions, informed by their own visions and undergirded by their own cultural values, morals, guiding principles, reasoning, and sense of justice (see Hoxie 2012). No matter how uneven the playing field has been, American Indian leaders, advocates, writers, and activists have long resisted all forms of American expansionism and have asserted themselves and their positions, whether in tribal delegations to Washington, treaty negotiations, military councils, U.S. courts, newspapers, the classroom, or on the lecture circuit. Since the country's earliest days, American Indians and the United States have been working out, in one fashion or another, the status of their unique relationship, and they have been working out just how the United States' most cherished values of liberty and equality apply to Native nations. In light of this morally, politically, and militarily entangled history, viewing U.S. emblems of national identity that employ American Indian imagery is deeply illuminating.

The roots of national identity, as revealed in imagery of American Indians, predate even the colonial history of the United States. Most New World Spanish, English, French, Swedish, and Dutch colonists' beliefs concerning the cultural differences between American Indians and themselves were accepted as preordained, absolute truths by British American colonists. These European assumptions have their own deep histories, which extend back to the Age of Discovery. Sixteenth-century Europe was stunned by its encounter with the New World. Neither the Americas nor its inhabitants fit into Biblical understandings of the world, nor into any understandings of it passed down from classical antiquity (Grafton [1992] 1995, 212). Renaissance thinkers had to redraw their maps, rethink their theology, rewrite their encyclopedias and history books—and come to an understanding of the indigenous peoples of the Americas. By the seventeenth and early eighteenth centuries, Europeans accepted the primacy of American Indians in the Western Hemisphere, at least to the degree that European rulers were not only theologically but also diplomatically and militarily preoccupied with what that primacy meant for themselves. They realized that Indians would affect their efforts to not only claim land and extract wealth from it but also impede the colonial ambitions of rival nations (Havard 2001).

By the second half of the eighteenth century, the situation of British American colonists in Native North America was fundamentally different from that of European colonists—at least in one crucial respect. No longer willing to be administered from afar, American colonists—the Founding Fathers and the first generation of Americans—had to develop ways of interacting closely with diverse Native nations and communities. During the Revolutionary War, some Native peoples fought with the patriots, and others with the redcoats. Some were powerful and held vast territories, while others were devastated by the war, including the search-and-burn tactics that were a part of the violence. Some were members of intertribal alliances that posed a serious threat to Americans; others controlled lucrative trade networks that were vital to the fledgling American economy.

Owing to the increasingly fraught relationship between Britain and the American colonists, the association of American Indians with the New World gradually took on a new dimension for a key and influential segment of the American revolutionary generation. In a significant shift, these Americans no longer thought of American Indians quite so simply as the exotic "other." Ideas about fundamental cultural differences remained in play, but important patriots began to appropriate the British symbol for the Daughters of Britannia (the American colonies). The symbol was an image of a so-called Indian Princess (see pages 46 and 52). The patriots coupled this and other images of American Indians with the Enlightenment concept of liberty—and, symbolically, with themselves (Olson 1991, 113). This new connotation layered onto American Indians helped clarify for the colonists and early Americans the sharp philosophical and political distinctions they were beginning to draw between themselves and Europeans—that is, peoples burdened by monarchies and subject to tyrannical rule.

The association, however, was not based solely on abstractions. Many early Americans noticed aspects of American Indian societies that resonated with them. Particularly important was the superficial, yet key, observation that American

Indian societies were not only untainted by monarchies but also relatively small (that is, ideally sized) and governed by consensus. Thus, when crucial distinctions needed to be drawn, the imagery of American Indians figured prominently in colonial Americans' attempts to establish and define for themselves the intellectual foundation of a republican democracy.

The United States' reliance on American Indian imagery to define itself has taken numerous intellectual twists and turns. From the days of Paul Revere and the patriots, ideas equating American Indians with individual liberty and self-government persisted, but during the late eighteenth through twentieth centuries, emerging ideas related to the country's sense of its national destiny were layered onto earlier uses of the imagery. Nonetheless, a commitment to revolutionary ideals (e.g., the belief that people should govern themselves) kept alive as a model an idealized version of American Indian society—even as the United States asserted its national power over more and more actual Native nations. Throughout U.S. history, real and imaginary relations between Americans and American Indians have existed—and both are embedded in the U.S. government's official and semiofficial uses of American Indian imagery. A close examination of the imagery reveals far more about the United States than it does about American Indians. It shows a country that has been preoccupied with defining what is American and has never been able to escape the question of how to practice its professed democratic ideals in its relationship with American Indians. It shows a country that has long grappled with how to extend the notion of human rights within its national borders, when the borders were knowingly drawn around those of Native nations that had no intention of relinquishing their sovereignty.

• • • •

Like language, imagery is a mode of signification. It is a vehicle through which the world—as construed by the creator and disseminator of the imagery—is represented. Like other cultural signs, imagery is motivated (Barthes [1957] 1972, 126–27). The reflections in this book proceed from the premise that the United States' continuous use of American Indian imagery in its national emblems is part of a deeply significant visual system of communication rooted in history. Since the images in the following pages are presented chronologically, it quickly becomes evident that some have great staying power. But, as images are historically as well as culturally constituted, they have been imbued with different meanings by different individuals at different times.

The first image discussed in this book (page 27) is believed to be one of the earliest visual representations of American Indians (Sturtevant 1976, 420; Feest 1984, 85 and 2014, 296–97). The woodcut shows an almost nude figure wearing a plumed skirt and a stand-up feather headdress. Dated 1505, it was used with little variation in any of its details for the next three hundred years. But, while many of its original meanings remained intelligible and even important, the image was nonetheless overlaid through time with connotations that took on more relevance and even greater significance for subsequent generations. An interplay of meanings emerged. What meanings took hold at any given time depended not only on who was deploying the image as well as where it was deployed, but also with what other images it was associated. In other words, the meanings associated with the seemingly static image depended on the system of signs in which it was used. For a sign-system is what gives specific imagery its clarity for its creators and intended audience, and a sign-system is what allows the imagery to resonate anew.

In contrast to the longevity of single images that reappear through time and take on different meanings, other, similarly employed imagery of American Indians could vary greatly but still read as symbolic signs with the same clear meanings. Seventeenth- and eighteenth-century European map cartouches were typically ornate panels, shaped as scrolls, containing the map's title, year, and other information as well as an elaborate figurative scene. To borrow an expression used by the semiotician Umberto Eco in a different context, European cartouches of this period are "mirrors of imperial society" (Eco 1989, 6). Cartouches on European maps of the New World embodied intentionally obvious imagery expressing European moral attitudes toward American Indians and, as one might expect, grandiloquent expressions of European designs on Indian territories. While the visual form of American Indians in map cartouches could vary greatly, the images nonetheless consistently signified European concepts of American Indian–ness within a restricted context and, moreover, the relations between European and Native nations—as understood by individual European powers.

For the nascent United States, American Indian imagery continued to be regarded as an especially useful means of expressing fundamental beliefs and geopolitical intentions. But in short order the United States' use of the imagery was shaped by its unique history. It reflected core U.S. values and the government's real-time relationships with American Indians. For the United States, imagery of American Indians has conveyed perennially useful meanings. But ultimately the remarkably multivalent imagery has symbolically expressed the difficult and complex social and political relations existing between the U.S. government and American Indian peoples at any given time. Or it has masked them—even when representations of American Indians were being erected as icons. Visual modes of signification can easily serve as artifice, for they are literally "ideas-in-form" (Barthes [1957] 1972, 112). They can falsify. Thus, in looking at the United States' use of American Indian imagery, we are glimpsing not necessarily history per se but rather, prevailing political and cultural concepts. What is most significant about these concepts as embodied in official, concrete, visual expressions of national identity is their "social *usage*" (ibid., 109; italics in the original), or precisely how, when, and why the imagery's highly charged meanings were transmitted by the U.S. government to the American people and countries abroad. One should bear in mind that while the emblems of national identity examined in this book were made, for the most part, under the aegis of federal departments or agencies, some of the individuals responsible for their creation were at the center of power, while others worked at the fringes. The more we understand about how all these emblems of national identity that pervade civic life and speak to power and display were created, the better we can understand why American Indian imagery constantly reappears on them.

None of the images in the following pages evoke a sense of rapid execution. Virtually all of them have genuine artistic merit. Most were created by accomplished engravers, printers, painters, sculptors, silversmiths, photographers, or glass workers who were sought out for their talents. Others were awarded commissions through competitions juried by distinguished statesmen, citizens, and fellow artists. What fascinates in their work is not the rehashing of tropes (i.e., noble savage or vanishing Indian) but the ingenuity of the imagery and how it speaks to what was novel and urgent when it was created. The imagery calls for close inspection. Each image must be understood within its own history as well as its historical milieu, and each as the result of deliberative decisions. The execution conveys serious thinking and, at times, a remarkable shift in attitudes.

Some imagery suggests Renaissance humanism and employs seemingly benign New World motifs that nonetheless immediately signaled non-Christian (i.e., uncivilized and savage) to its contemporaneous European or American viewers. Some imagery speaks to a nation in search of its identity. Some speaks to the creation of a republic that was determined to break up Native nations. Some images speak to a national euphoria in the aftermath of a closed frontier, and others to a nation assured of its power. Some imagery speaks to a nation in search of a cultural pedigree. Some works speak to the specter of capitalist hegemony, while others show an acceptance of pluralism, seeming to welcome the diversity of American life. More often than not, the assembled images are threaded with a constant misreading of the "other." But in all of it, what matters most is the wide spectrum of images that reflect the United States' constant reexamining and re-articulation of how its relationship with American Indians relates to its core values. Intentionally or not, the images reflect how American Indians fit into the United States' democratic experiment at critical moments in its history. And they mirror the United States' own understanding of the importance of its treatment of people within its borders.

• • • •

The meanings embedded in U.S. imagery of American Indians can often appear paradoxical, counterintuitive, and contradictory to one another—and even contradictory to their eras' prevailing attitudes toward American Indians. What intrigues is how often a range of connotations is encapsulated in a single image, how various images of American Indians have been made to mean and mean again; and how so many representations of American Indians seemed to be, to borrow an apt expression from cultural critic and theorist Dick Hebdige (1979, 13), "shrouded in common sense," or made to seem natural or obvious. To be sure, taken together official and semiofficial use of American Indian imagery represents the United States' ambivalence toward American Indians. Still, what remains important is that the United States throughout its history has regarded itself as a country engaged in democracy; its relations, real and imaginary, with American Indians speak powerfully to this critical fact. The United States has always had to confront its relationship with American Indians—whether or not it has ever invested in understanding them as anything more than abstractions.

While this book shows how American assumptions about American Indians are rooted in European thought and imagery, its focus is on a country that has long been grappling with itself, specifically with the question of how ideals of liberty and equality apply to different people. These people include American Indians, who are singled out in the U.S. Constitution alongside foreign nations and state governments as having inherent powers of self-government, and who, for more than two hundred years, have been trying to shatter lingering assumptions that have been detrimental to their interests and well-being. In the United States, the Constitution is supposed to be what holds people together. It defines what human rights, or "liberty and equality for all," means in the United States. The imagery of American Indians from the Age of Discovery to the present that I discuss in the following pages reveals how the United States' associations with American Indians cannot be dislodged from associations dating back four centuries. More important, however, it brings to light how deeply embedded American Indians are in the United States' sense of itself as a nation. Whether or not Americans and American Indians have ever been in lockstep, the imagery exposes how tightly interconnected they are in the effort to uphold the United States' democratic inheritance.

ESSAYS

SAILING UNDER THE FLAG OF PORTUGAL, the Italian explorer, navigator, and cartographer Amerigo Vespucci inadvertently explored coastal Brazil in 1501 and 1502, not fully realizing until his return to Lisbon that he had set foot in the "New World." Vespucci wrote vividly and published often about his voyages; for this reason, it is possible that the "fourth continent" was named after him rather than Christopher Columbus (Grafton [1992] 1995, 83). Vespucci described his explorations of the land now known as Brazil in two letters, which were published together in late 1502 or 1503 as a pamphlet titled *Mundus Novus.* His account was vivid but fictitious. It was reprinted in 1505 and illustrated with an equally fantastical woodcut by Johann Froschauer that had a long-lasting impact on how indigenous peoples of the Americas were represented visually in Europe. The German caption that accompanies the Froschauer illustration translates as:

> This figure represents to us the people and island which have been discovered by the Christian King of Portugal or by his subjects. The people are thus naked, handsome, brown, well-shaped in body, their heads, necks, arms, private parts, feet of men and women are little covered in feathers. The men also have many precious stones in their faces and breasts. No one also has anything, but all things are in common. And the men [have] as wives those who please them, be they mothers, sisters, or friends, therein they make no distinction. They also fight with each other. They also eat each other, even those who are slain, and hang the flesh of them in smoke. They become one hundred and thirty years old. And have no government.

In addition to showing cannibalism, the woodcut illustrates indigenous men with beards, another made-up observation, since Native men typically have less facial hair than Europeans and generally do not grow it. The bearded men appear to the right in the wood-block print, while in the top center is part of a person "hanging like pork in a European butcher's shop," as Vespucci was purported to have said in describing a scene he claimed to have observed on his voyage (ibid.). To the far left is a figure, perhaps a woman, eating a human arm. Almost as soon as the woodcut was published, near-nudity and cannibalism became two of the most common visual conventions in Europe for depicting the indigenous peoples of the Western Hemisphere—so much so that they became emblematic (ibid., 110). Vespucci's observations of flora and fauna that had been unknown to Europeans and his description of the Southern Cross constellation, also newly revealed to Europeans, contributed to an idea that indigenous peoples across the Atlantic Ocean lived outside the norms of anything recognizable as (civilized) human society (ibid., 84–85).

Contemporary researchers have surmised that the people Vespucci met in Brazil were Tupinambá Indians, not because of their purported cannibalism or beards, but because of the feather headdresses, bustles, collars, anklets, and armlets that Vespucci described and Froschauer depicted (Sturtevant 1976, 420). Their plumed

Johann Froschauer (dates unknown). *Tupinambás of Coastal Brazil,* **1505.** Woodcut published in *Mundus Novus,* 1505. Courtesy of the Granger Collection, New York

skirts are believed to have been yet another fabrication, this time by Froschauer (Sturtevant 1976, 420), but the other articles of attire are typical of Tupinambá dress. Clothing was one of the most important ways of illustrating cultural diversity in sixteenth-century Europe (Feest 2014, 289). This might well explain why the plumed skirts and stand-up feather headdresses featured in Froschauer's wood block would become such widespread means of depicting indigenous peoples of the Americas—and of emphasizing their supposed differences (e.g., heathenism, cannibalism) from Europeans. These visual conventions lasted for a remarkably long time. Even American colonists and the Founding Fathers adopted them to depict North American Indians (see pages 50 and 66).

IN 1588, THE FRANCO-FLEMISH ENGRAVER AND PUBLISHER Theodore de Bry began to publish what eventually became a thirteen-volume book titled *America*. Between 1590 and 1618, it was printed in several languages, and each volume included engraved scenes of the "New World." Most of the illustrations were based upon those of other artists. De Bry never visited the Americas. Nonetheless, his publication, particularly its engravings, provided a European audience with what they considered to be their first authentic, comprehensive glimpse of the New World's indigenous peoples (Grafton [1992] 1995, 128). Despite his lack of firsthand knowledge of his subject, de Bry's purpose in publishing his tome was to further his Protestant theological agenda.

De Bry routinely embellished other artists' work when he republished their earlier illustrations, and he was not averse to creating his own scenes of life in Native North America. The title page of volumes 3 and 4 of *America* portrays American Indian men and women as cannibals and idolaters. To fully underscore his point that the indigenous peoples of the Americas existed outside European norms, he placed them, incongruously, in a classically inspired architectural setting. From antiquity to de Bry's day, placing statues of saints and rulers in niches was an artistic convention used to honor those individuals. By placing American Indians in niches, de Bry portrayed them not simply as culturally different but also, quite effectively, as sharing no common ground with Europeans.

The idea that peoples living well beyond one's borders were barbarous cannibals can be traced back to works of classical antiquity, including that of Pliny the Elder (AD 23–79). Such beliefs circulated widely throughout medieval and Renaissance Europe (ibid., 108), as did the related idea that distant peoples were idolaters. With all the power that a master engraver (he was also a goldsmith) could impart to his visual medium, de Bry projected onto American Indians via his title page these widely shared sixteenth-century European beliefs.

Moreover, de Bry's highly influential work interpreted the existence of American Indians on a distant continent in terms of his own religious beliefs concerning man's expulsion from Paradise. De Bry's intent was to portray American Indians not only as living in ignorance of Christianity but also as "irredeemably lost" (ibid., 128) because they had fallen from grace. De Bry's *America* and the monstrous race of American Indians he depicted, including on the highly imaginative title pages of volumes 3 and 4, reached an international audience that was also well versed in biblical history—and fully receptive to de Bry's efforts to tie American Indians to it (ibid., 128–29).

Theodore de Bry (1528–1598). Title pages in *America*, vols. 3 and 4, 1592. Engraving. Courtesy of the John Carter Brown Library at Brown University, Providence, Rhode Island

Dritte Buch Americæ,

Darinn

Braſilia durch Johann Staden von

Homberg auß Heſſen / auß eigener erfahrung
in Teutſch beſchrieben. Item Hiſtoria der Schiffart
Ioannis Lerij in Braſilien / welche er ſelbſt publiciert hat /
jetzt von Newem verteutſcht / Durch Teucrium
Annæum Priuatum, C.

Vom Wilden vnerhörtem weſen der Innwo-
ner / von allerley frembden Gethieren vnd Ge-
wächſen / ſampt einem Colloquio, in der
Wilden Sprach.

Alles von Newem mit künſtlichen Figuren in Kupffer
geſtochen vnd an Tag geben / Durch Dieterich Bry von
Lüttich / jetzt Burger zu Franckfurt
am Mayn.

1 5 9 3.

1 6 2 4

Venales reperiütur in officina
Theodori de Bry.

IN 1662, THE MASTER DUTCH CARTOGRAPHER AND PRINTER Joan Blaeu published a lavish and highly coveted twelve-volume atlas that aimed to provide up-to-date knowledge about all parts of the known world, including those parts that Europeans were encountering for the first time during the Age of Exploration (fifteenth through seventeenth centuries). At the time, atlases were considered the major new source of knowledge, the Dutch were regarded as indomitable seafarers, and the Blaeu family was esteemed as one of Europe's finest mapmakers and publishers of atlases.

With Europeans circumnavigating the globe, the "known world" could no longer be explained by the texts that Europeans had depended upon, namely, the Bible, encyclopedias, and certain works of classical antiquity. Convincing and reassuring, these texts had seemingly summed up all the world's knowledge (Grafton [1992] 1995, 13–58). Beginning with Christopher Columbus's "discovery" of the "New World," however, encounters with indigenous peoples in the Western Hemisphere raised a wealth of unsettling and challenging questions for Europeans. As decades became centuries, thinkers across Europe sought to understand from religious, historical, political, economic, and scientific angles not only the existence of a "fourth continent" but also its inhabitants.

Beginning in the seventeenth century, for example, naturalists sailed to the New World to observe, sketch, and paint plants, animals, birds, and insects previously unknown to Europeans. In his twelve-volume atlas, Blaeu attempted to assemble the vast range of this emerging information (ibid., 242–43). But while the Old World was using new scientific methods to document the New World, Europe was also steeped in traditional ways of rendering the world meaningful, and Europeans still applied those traditions to their attempts to understand the New World's flora, fauna, and peoples.

Allegory, a way of representing abstract ideas or qualities in a concrete or visual form, was particularly common during the Renaissance (Clarke 2010, 7). On the title page of deluxe editions of his *Geographica* volume, Blaeu presented an allegory of the New World as an American Indian huntress. She is holding a bow and arrow and is surrounded by phenomena found only in the Western Hemisphere, including, possibly, a crocodile-like creature called a caiman. An image of an American Indian woman was, by this time, widely employed by Europeans to personify the fourth continent (Olson 1991, 75). In his representation, however, Blaeu was intending to express something beyond the usual symbolism of this allegory.

Blaeu's engraving was based upon a drawing created for him by Dutch artist Nicolaes Berchem the Elder (1620–1683). Berchem specialized in landscapes, and

Joan Blaeu (1596–1673), *Allegory of America,* **1662.** Engraving published in *Geographica*, vol. 11. Courtesy of Dartmouth College Library, Hanover, New Hampshire; item located in the Rauner Special Collections Library

in his drawing he "reconfigured the New World allegory for a Dutch context by including a detailed setting alluding to trade and religion" (Metropolitan Museum of Art 2016). To be sure, Berchem was reworking one of the first European visual representations of American Indians ever produced—that of the coastal South American Tupinambá Indians illustrated in Amerigo Vespucci's *Mundus Novus* of 1505 (see page 27.) Berchem dispensed with the feather collar, armbands, and anklets but privileged the stand-up feather headdress and plumed skirt of the earlier work. Berchem then added to America's attributes a bow, arrows, and quivers. While bows, arrows, and quivers may seem synonymous with American Indians to those who grew up on Hollywood Westerns, that association would not have been in the minds of Blaeu's late-seventeenth-century audience.

Berchem/Blaeu's allegory is hypersymbolic, meaning that it conflates several concepts in one image: the fourth continent; Diana, the Roman goddess of the hunt; and Amazon women. During the Renaissance, when Diana was not depicted emerging from her outdoor bath she was often shown with a double-arc bow, a quiver, and arrows, sometimes with the spoils of her hunt at her feet. The Amazon, a race of women warriors, had been well established in Greek mythology, and Amazons often appear in Renaissance as well as ancient Greek art. The Spanish explorer and conquistador Francisco de Orellana reported encountering and even fighting with Amazons in the South American interior during his expedition in 1542. He also sailed the length of the great river that he eventually named after those Amazons. Shortly after Orellana returned to Spain and reported his ordeals to the Spanish Crown, nearly nude Amazons carrying bows began to be depicted on European maps of South America.

Berchem/Blaeu's *America*, equipped with a bow and a quiver full of arrows, has one foot on the head of a European that is pierced with an arrow. The Rauner Library traces the origin of the arrow-pierced head and the caiman at America's feet to an illustration in the 1618 edition of Cesare Ripa's *Nova Iconologia*. According to staff at the Rauner Library, late Renaissance artists and poets used the *Nova Iconologia* as a source for abstract concepts and associated visual imagery (Rauner Library 2011). The head shown in the engraving—an image most Europeans accepted as based upon truth—is meant to depict what remains of a European who has been devoured by a cannibal. Other scenes in Bercham/Blaeu's allegory show silver or gold being mined, a reference to the wealth Europeans were seeking in the New World. In the clouds from left to right are heathenism being dispatched by a conquistador, Christianity being brought to receptive Indians, and the continent being labeled America by cherubs. In a distant harbor, European ships are poised to be loaded with New World wealth extracted from the land. In its focus as well as its details, Berchem/Blaeu's depiction of an American Indian woman is freighted with symbolic meanings that have little to do with indigenous American women but speak volumes to European designs on the continent.

Alexis-Hubert Jaillot (1632?–1712). *Amerique septentrionale divisée en ses principales parties,* **1674** (detail). Engraved, hand-colored map. Courtesy of the Library of Congress Geography and Map Division G3300 1694 .J2

THIS FRENCH MAP SHOWS THAT BY 1694 six European powers—France, Spain, England, Sweden, Denmark, and Holland—were vying to extend their imperial reach and had laid claim to virtually all Native North America. In the upper left corner of the map is an elaborate cartouche. At the top center of the cartouche's scrollwork are the French royal crest and crown. On either side are perched two parrots, birds indigenous to the Western Hemisphere and often used by Europeans to symbolize the "New World." In the lower part of the scrollwork appear an armadillo on the left and a monkey on the right, two animals that also symbolized the New World. Two figures emerging out of the scrollwork are wearing plumed skirts and stand-up feather headdresses; they signify the Americas' indigenous peoples.

That the human figures are presented as decorative motifs can be read in at least two ways. First, their presence may simply reflect a skilled engraver's indulgence in the exuberant French baroque style. The oddly treated pair of American Indians is reminiscent of (and may be related to) the European tradition of illuminated manuscripts, in which figures (sometimes fabulous creatures known as drolleries) were artistically inserted into initial capital letters at the beginning of gospels. Or they may mimic the Baroque custom of carving term figures (busts from the torso up) into furniture legs or arm supports.

Alexis-Hubert Jaillot (1632?–1712). *Amerique septentrionale divisée en ses principales parties,* **1674.**
Engraved, hand-colored map. Courtesy of the Library of Congress Geography and Map Division G3300
1694 .J2

A second, more historical reading of the two American Indians embedded in the scrollwork may be as the intentional expression of France's power and control in the New World. The baroque style, prevalent in Western Europe from about 1590 to 1750, was especially embraced in France. The French monarchy supported and encouraged it as an expression of France's grandeur and triumphalism on the world stage. That support is most famously embodied in the architecture and gardens of the Palace of Versailles, but the style also found dramatic expression in the "lesser" French decorative arts.

During the Age of Exploration (fifteenth through seventeenth centuries), European map cartouches served as more than a place for identifying the land being mapped and when, where, and by whom the map was created. Cartouches from the period almost always included scenic imagery expressing, obliquely or not, valuable information about the attitudes and beliefs of the map's creators. As such, the maps were conceived and received, at least in part, as narrative geography. The narrative communicated in the cartouche on this map appears to show that American Indians—at least those who lived in the vast territory that the French monarch Louis XIV had claimed by 1694—have been caught up in the orb of French power. French colonies multiplied during Louis XIV's reign, and French explorers in the Americas had made several important "discoveries" in their monarch's name. But by 1694, France and Britain were fighting intermittently for control of North America, and both nations were seeking Native trading and military alliances. Here, the visual representations of American Indians wearing plumed skirts and stand-up feather headdresses signify not only the New World in general but also the North American territory—most of modern-day Canada, the Great Lakes region, and northern New England—to which France laid claim. In its desire to control the fur trade, the French monarchy may have imagined it controlled vast regions of Native North America in the late seventeenth century. In fact, American Indians were a demographic majority seeking to maintain autonomy while aligning with the Native or European peoples who best suited their interests.

DURING THE AGE OF EXPLORATION (fifteenth through seventeenth centuries), Europeans created numerous maps in their attempts to accurately define land masses, coastlines, major waterways, and the interiors of continents they were seeing for the first time. During the seventeenth century, especially, Amsterdam was one of Europe's most important ports and commercial centers. This extraordinary map of the Atlantic seaboard from Virginia to Maine, made by Dutch cartographer Nicolaes Visscher I in 1656 and reprinted in 1685 by his son, has been called the "best and most complete representation we have of [the colony of] New Netherland during the Dutch period. [I]t may be correctly described as a scientific map" (Stokes 1915, 118). It may also be described as a European (Dutch) cultural artifact.

Seventeenth-century Europeans held deep beliefs concerning individuals who lived in towns and those who did not. Since the Middle Ages, the idea of the "wild man of the woods" had captured European imaginations and appeared frequently in art and literature (Bernheimer 1952). The concept defined those who did not live in towns as lacking in the habits and manners that distinguished town dwellers. Those in towns imagined that people inhabiting the European forests wore little clothing and had no notion of farming or knowledge of God—prerequisites for living a civilized life.

In addition to the pervasive "wild man of the woods" belief, seventeenth-century Europeans also held the more ancient opinion that those who lived beyond the borders of their countries lacked civi-

Nicolaes Visscher II (1649–1702). *Novi Belgii Novæque Angliæ: nec non partis Virginiæ tabula multis in locis emendata*, 1685. Engraved, hand-colored map. Courtesy of the Library of Congress Geography and Map Division G3715 169- .V5 TIL

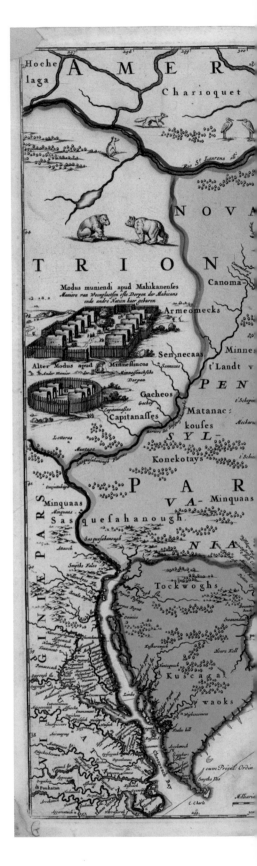

CÆ SEPTEN

Matouôwesarini

NOVÆ FRANCIÆ

PARS

La Grand Riviere de Canada   Mont Royal   Lac St Piere   Quebec   de Orleans

Rio de Guenas

Rio St Laurentius

Groote Val

NOVA ANGLIA
ofte
Ammo
cangen
NIEUW ENGE
LANDT by
d'Jnwoonders genaemt

Tadoussac

ELGICA   sive NIEUW

Quebecq

Lacus
Irocoisi
ensis
efte
Meer
der
Irocoisen

Horikans

Kennebeka

Anco:
cisco

Mackwaas

Mahikans

Nawaas

Sequins

Coultekock

Nyser

Makimanes

Quirepeys

Pachami

Quyropey

Swanoys

Siwanoys

Moricans

Pequtoo=

Wapanoos

Horicans

Noort
Zee

Zuyder
Zee

Cape Cod
Wit hoeck
Cape Iames

Mackwaas

Waoranecks

Wecke

Wapingues

Waranawankongs

COLONIE
VAN
Tappaans
DE HEER NEDRE

't Lange Eylandt alias Matouwacs
Iorck Shire.

NEDER   LANDT   nu

IEW IORCK

Mackwaas

Matovancons

Aquuachu Soques

Ermonex

Sanhicans

MAR   DEL   NORT

Rivier eertyts de stat Amsterdam

Canioz sive Naviculo e corticibus arborum

Naris ex arboris trunco igne excavata

Foederati

NOVI BELGII
NOVÆQUE ANGLIÆ NEC NON
PARTIS
VIRGINIÆ TABULA
multis in locis emendata
per Nicolaum Visscher
Nunc apud Petr. Schenk Jun.

NIEUW AMSTERDAM
of t Eylant Manhattans

A. Net Fort B. de Kerck C. de Wintmolen D. dese Vlagge wert op gehaelt als daer Schepen in de Haven komen. E. t'gevangen huys F. de N. Generaels huys G. t Gorecke H. de Kaeck I. Compagnies Pachuys K. Stadts Herbergh

Map Division
Library of Congress

L169-J

37

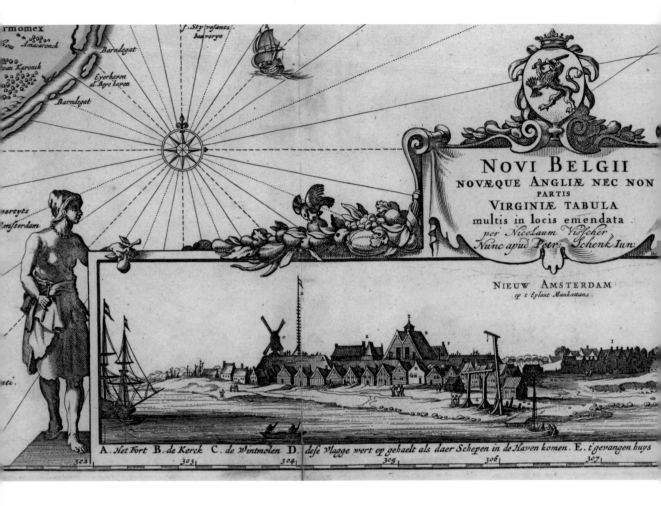

A. Het Fort   B. de Kerck   C. de Wintmolen   D. dese Vlagge wert op gehaelt als daer Schepen in de Haven komen.   E. t' gevangen huys

lized manners. This view is found in the writings of the Greek historian Herodotus (ca. 484–ca. 425 BC), who has been called the world's first historian. Herodotus is credited with calling attention to the fact that people living in different areas have different customs. But he is also singled out as one of the classical writers most responsible for identifying non-Greeks as barbarians (Rowe 1965, 2).

While Visscher's remarkable map locates numerous Native settlements by name and includes two detailed drawings of palisaded villages identified as Mahican, it also locates many Dutch, Swedish, and English settlements. But taking pride of place inside its cartouche is a view of New Amsterdam (present-day New York City), comfortably nestled into a cleared coastal landscape. One of its tallest buildings, as identified in its legend, is *de Kerck* (the church).

That New Amsterdam is flanked by American Indians on the outer edges of the cartouche may be read as acknowledging Native primacy in the "New World," but it may also be understood to reflect the European belief that Christian town dwell-

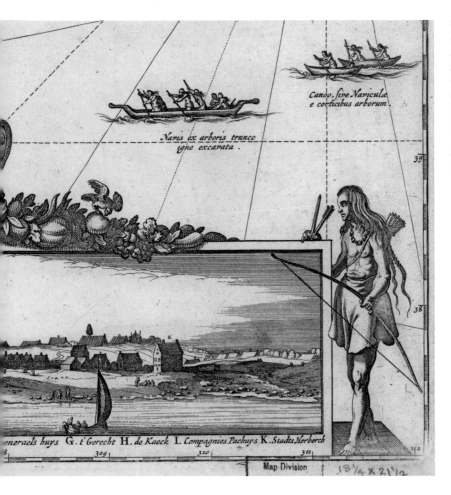

Nicolaes Visscher II (1649–1702). *Novi Belgii Novæque Angliæ: nec non partis Virginiæ tabula multis in locis emendata,* **1685** (detail). Engraved, hand-colored map. Courtesy of the Library of Congress Geography and Map Division G3715 169- .V5 TIL

ers (and seafarers) were superior to the New World forest dwellers. That American Indians are forest dwellers is clearly signified by the bow, arrows, and quiver that the Indian on the right carries as well as by the rude Indian settlements shown on the map. In the cartouche, the size of the apparently prosperous and orderly Dutch village, with its well-constructed buildings and busy port, signals the assumption that in clearing the wilderness, spreading settlements, and controlling international trade, Europeans were vastly superior to American Indians. This highly detailed and informative map of New England effortlessly normalizes, in an American context, beliefs that had held sway in Europe for at least two thousand years (Barthes [1957] 1972, 140).

BY THE EIGHTEENTH CENTURY, a near-nude figure wearing a plumed skirt and a stand up feather headdress had become a widespread visual convention for depicting any "New World" American Indian—whether male, female, child, adult, or from any part of the Western Hemisphere. English tobacconists employed the figure specifically to represent a strain of tobacco (*Nicotiana tabacum*) that Jamestown colonist John Rolfe had cultivated from seeds he obtained in the Caribbean, possibly Trinidad. The tobacco, well adapted to the rich bottomland of the James River, had a taste the English found extremely pleasant. Rolfe exported his first crop to England in 1613; by 1640, London was importing a million and a half pounds of tobacco from Virginia every year. Virtually overnight, tobacco grown in colonial Virginia became an enormously profitable cash crop for the English and hugely important to the English economy.

Smoking leaf tobacco in clay pipes became fashionable throughout Europe during the seventeenth century, but it was a costly pastime that tended to be restricted to the wealthier classes. As quickly as the Jamestown colonists realized that cultivating tobacco could be lucrative, they also figured out that it was labor intensive. Enslaved Africans were brought to Jamestown as early as 1619 (Wolfe 2015). The profitability of tobacco led an increasing number of colonists during the 1620s and 1630s to demand tracts of land along the York River, which they quickly converted into tobacco plantations (Rountree and Turner [2002] 2005, 149; Salmon and Salmon 2013). The virtual explosion of these plantations resulted in wars with the Powhatan Confederacy of coastal Algonquian Indians. The first lasted from 1610 to 1614, the second from 1622 to 1628, and the third from 1644 to 1646. All three wars led to the perilous decline of the Powhatan population. By 1675, the English controlled the Virginia coastal plain, surviving Powhatans were living on the first reservation established in North America, and enslaved Africans working on plantations outnumbered English indentured servants by four to one (Wolfe 2015).

In this English tobacco-paper/advertisement, enslaved African workers are shown filling three barrels with tobacco under the vigilant eye of an English colonist, who is distinguished by a waistcoat that flares at the waist and reaches to his knees. While the sun beats down on the workers, an Indian, recognizable by his stand-up feather headdress, holds a parasol to shade the colonist. The two large American Indians in the foreground who frame the scene also wear stand-up feather headdresses; their plumed skirts are clearly visible.

The two large figures, smoking pipes and holding twists of tobacco, fill the picture plane. But their prominence belies the geopolitical reality of the Chesapeake Bay region. The Indian holding the parasol is unmistakably submissive to the

Rolls's Best Virginia **tobacco advertisement, 1700s.** Woodblock. Courtesy of the British Museum, London. Heal, 117.137 © The Trustees of the British Museum

colonist. The two large Indians, who are entirely independent of the activity in the middle ground, do not represent the Powhatan Indians who had been decimated by the English and whose survivors had been driven onto a reservation. They signify on this tobacco-paper advertisement the source (colonial Virginia) and quality (*Nicotiana tabacum*) of the tobacco being packed into barrels for export to London. In short, they denote the wealth Britain sought and found in the New World.

THIS MAP OF "THE WHOLE WORLD WITH THE TRADE WINDS" made in 1732 by the London-based Dutch cartographer Herman Moll speaks to Europeans' growing engagement in and reliance on maritime trade during the eighteenth century. During this time, increased knowledge of sea routes and trade winds, in addition to the development of large, wide-hulled trading vessels, enabled Europeans to establish trade routes across the Atlantic and Pacific Oceans.

Improved European trade with India and China as well as exchanges in Native North America among European colonists and American Indians led to global commerce. American Indians were themselves inveterate traders. With well-established trade routes dating back thousands of years, the exchange and innovation fostered by trade had always been integral to their history and culture. It should come as no surprise that American Indians did not remain on the sidelines of a burgeoning worldwide trade network but rather, were active agents in it.

American Indians' interest in exotic and even luxury global goods (textiles, including wool, silk, and cotton; jewelry, including silver gorgets, brooches, earrings, and armbands; and decorative embellishments such as glass beads) was satisfied by their ability to offer, in exchange, the natural resources the Europeans sought, especially deer hides and the pelts of beaver, marten, otter, and black fox. Even as American Indians endeavored to curtail European expansion in North America, many Native nations jockeyed to capitalize on trading opportunities with Europeans, establishing themselves as fur traders or vital middlemen. As historian James Axtell writes, "Clearly, the natives of eastern America controlled resources that were in demand in Europe" (2001, 107). Axtell further points out, for example, that in 1764 the southern colonies shipped more than eight hundred thousand pounds of deerskin to Europe (1997, 48). In exchange for that deerskin and various pelts, Southeast Indians demanded specific manufactured trade goods, most notably textiles. American Indians also acquired textiles though treaty negotiations. Treaties in Pennsylvania dating to the early eighteenth century, including a treaty negotiated in 1715 between the Pennsylvania Provincial Council and the Delaware, document that cloth was central to diplomatic negotiations (Johnson 2009, 116).

In North America, as throughout the world, textiles were one of the most important trade items by the eighteenth century (Peck 2013, 105–19). Not surprisingly then, by the time this English trade winds map was printed in 1732, American Indians along the Atlantic coast were wearing woven woolens perfected by the British, colorful silk fabric and ribbons imported from China and India, and patterned cotton, or calico, that originated in India. American Indians quickly absorbed global trade goods into their lifeways, and they integrated the goods into their design vocabularies and techniques of weaving, sewing, appliqué, and embroidery. In so doing, they created distinctive visual identities.

Eighteenth-century American Indian clothing seen in rare surviving examples as well as in European paintings and drawings demonstrates that indigenous peoples of North America living along the Atlantic coast were indisputably an integral part of a global trade network. Although American Indians were inveterate traders key to the Atlantic trade, determined negotiators and, inarguably, cosmopolitan dressers, European visual representations of them often remained unchanged from those of the sixteenth century. The American Indian figure in the lower left corner of this map is depicted wearing a stand-up feather headdress and a plumed skirt—a now two-century-old convention (see pages 27, 32). Its inclusion on *A new map of the whole world* is clearly intended to help convey the diversity of mankind Europeans were encountering as they traded throughout the world. But the figure speaks much more directly to Europe's unbending view of the Americas' indigenous peoples than to the diversity, desire for new trading opportunities, and cultural inventiveness of the American Indians that Europeans actually encountered in early eighteenth-century North America.

Herman Moll (1654?–1732). *A new map of the whole world with the trade winds according to ye latest and most exact observations,* **1732** (detail). Engraved, colored map. Published by Thomas Bowles. Courtesy of the Norman B. Leventhal Map Center at the Boston Public Library, Massachusetts

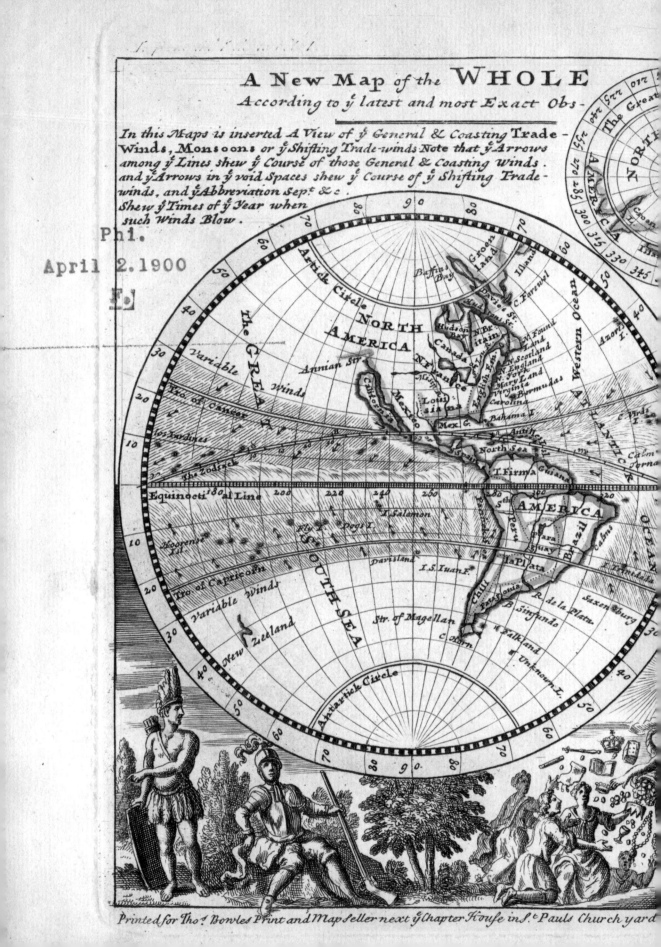

WORLD with the Trade winds

ervations By H. Moll Geographer

The Signs of the Zodiack, The First 6 are Northern, the other Southern Signs

♈ Aries . March	♌ Leo . Iuly	♐ Sagittaris . November
♉ Taurus . April	♍ Virgo . August	♑ Capricornus . Decemb.
♊ Gemini . May	♎ Libra . September	♒ Aquarius . Ianuary
♋ Cancer . Iune	♏ Scorpio . October	♓ Pisces . February

North Pole

Green L.
Green L.
N. Zembla
Parts Unknown
Dom. of Russia
GTARTARY
Dom. of Rvssia
Iesso I.
Str. of Jesso

EVROPE
Poland
ASIA
Yemur R.
Iapon
Bungo

Ireland
C. Clear
Britain
Swede
North C.
Denmark

Spain
Italy
Turky
Levant
China

Portugal
Str. Monco
Barbary
Canary I.
Mawoo
Med. Sea
Persia
Mogul
INDIA

Biledulgerid
Zara
Egypt
Arab
Bengal
Formosa
Ladrone I.
Philippina I.
Guam

Virde I.
Negroland
Niger R.
Nubia
Abissina
Borneo
Amadian
Celebs

AFRICA
Guinea
Ethiopia
C. Comorin
Ceylon or
Ethiopian or
EASTERN or
Sumatra
Sunda

Ascension
Congo
Nile
INDIAN OCEAN
Timor
N. Britain

St. Helena
Ethiopian Sea
Monomotapa
I. Mada gascar
New Holland
Carpentaria

C. of Good Hope
Denia I.
I. Amsterdam
Lewin Land

I. Tristan da Cunha

Dimen I.

South Pole

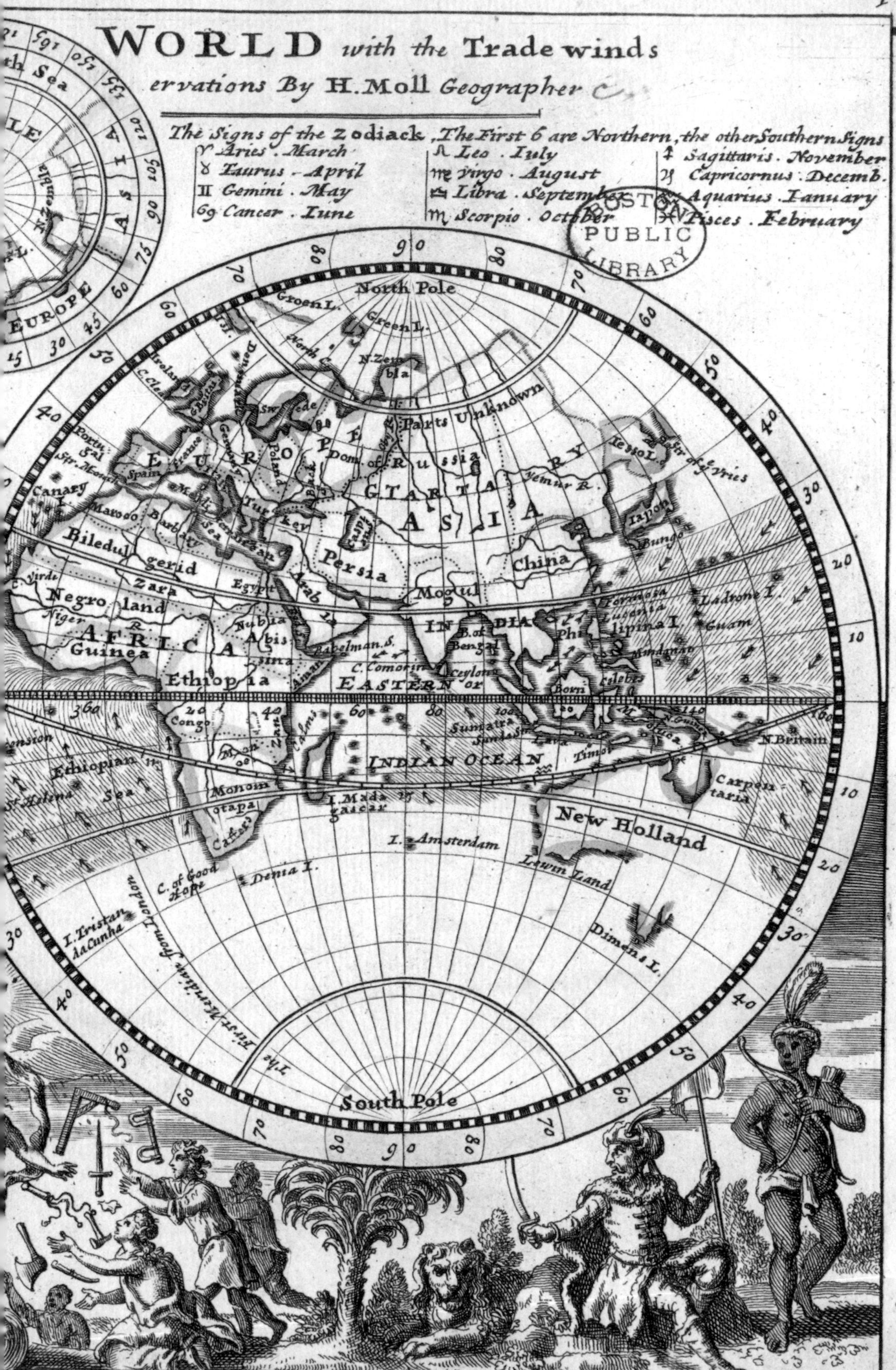

John Bowles Print and Map Seller at the Black Horse in Cornhill London.

PAUL REVERE'S COPPERPLATE ENGRAVING for the lantern-illuminated, oiled-paper obelisk that was constructed on Boston Common on May 22, 1766, to celebrate of the repeal of the Stamp Act of 1765 is all that remains of that triumphant and historic affair (Olson 1991, 110; Fischer 2005, 99–101). The Stamp Act of 1765, which had been passed by the British Parliament, imposed a duty on newspapers and legal and commercial documents in the British American colonies. Colonists considered this and other taxes (such as the tea tax) excessively burdensome. To add insult to injury, the taxes were levied by a distant legislature in which the colonies had no representation. Opposition to the Stamp Act was one of many rebellious stances colonists took that precipitated the American Revolutionary War. Quite unintentionally, the oiled-paper obelisk went up in flames during the excitement of the evening.

Revere, a skilled silversmith, goldsmith, and printmaker, was an ardent patriot and politically active in the Freemasons as well as the Sons of Liberty (Fischer 1994, 13–22). Thought to date to the Middle Ages, the Freemasons formed a fraternal organization that took root in the American colonies and would claim among its members George Washington, Benjamin Franklin, and thirteen other signers of the Constitution. At Freemason meetings, Revere mingled with the gentlemen for whose tables he made tankards, bowls, and spoons. He shared their republican values and sought to enter their ranks, if only with a military appointment, but he was never so accepted (Skemp 1999, 370). Nonetheless, Revere maintained his revolutionary zeal, which perhaps found its fullest expression in the Sons of Liberty, a grassroots patriotic and fraternal organization known for its revolutionary acts leading up the American Revolutionary War.

Before the outbreak of the American Revolution, the British were publishing political engravings in France and the thirteen American colonies, as well as in Britain, that clearly expressed their deepening discontent with the colonies' rebelliousness. The British had long conceived of the colonies as the Daughters of Britannia, depicting them visually as a single Indian Princess. Increasingly, they depicted the princess as unruly, vulnerable, weak, or naïve (Olson 1991, 2). Americans, most notably Paul Revere and the Sons of Liberty, appropriated the pictorial language of Britain's political prints, including the Indian Princess image. In the patriots' hands, she became an image of strength, determination, justified rebellion, and, eventually, liberty.

Revere's engraved sketch for the oiled-paper obelisk erected to celebrate the repeal of the Stamp Act of 1765 is an important colonial American political print in which the symbol of the American Indian was invested with powerful new meanings. Revere produced several such prints for the *Royal American Magazine, or Universal Repository of Instruction and Amusement* (see page 53) and was clearly well versed in the pictorial language of British political prints. Across the top of his

Paul Revere (1735–1818). *A View of the Obelisk Erected under Liberty-Tree in Boston on the Rejoicings for the Repeal of the — Stamp Act, 1766* (restrike 1943). Engraving. Courtesy of the Library of Congress Prints and Photographs Division, LC-USZC4-4599

sketch is written, "A View of the Obelisk erected under Liberty Tree in Boston on the Rejoicings for the Repeal of the Stamp Act, 1766." Revere drew the portraits of four statesmen at the top of each side of the tapering obelisk.[1] Beneath each portrait is text, beneath which is an accompanying pictorial scene. The text expresses the patriots' love of liberty, distress at the thought of losing their liberty, the sense of Britain as a tyrannical foe and obstacle to that liberty, and their fervent belief in their cause.

Following a description of the iconography by scholar Lester C. Olson (1991, 110), reading from left to right, the first scene depicts a seated Indian Princess wearing a feathered skirt and stand-up feather headdress. Hovering above her is Liberty, holding a liberty pole and copy of the Stamp Act.[2] To their right, the British government, led by the devil, attempts to impose the Stamp Act. In the next scene, the Indian Princess genuflects before William Pitt, the British statesman who supported the colonists. Fame, holding a trumpet in one hand, hovers above, portending a favorable outcome for the patriots. The third scene depicts a tree with birds being rescued from a predator. The last scene depicts Liberty and the Indian Princess again appealing to their supporter, William Pitt.

Taken together, these four scenes make it clear that the colonists' grievances were not with the British Crown so much as with a British Parliament in which they had no representation and that was taxing them without their consent. The colonists believed that their British heritage entitled them to the same rights that British citizens living in England received (Olson 1991, 104). The scenes in this engraving make it even clearer that, in the hands of the revolutionary generation, American Indian imagery was being dramatically transformed into an emblem of liberty. The image of the American Indian, which the British had used to signify tobacco (the cash crop extracted from its Virginia colony) and later its thirteen American colonies (the Daughters of Britannia), had now become distinctly American, firmly associated with the rebels' fight for liberty. The association would become even stronger in the years to come (Fischer 2005, 140–44).

Paul Revere (1735–1818). *A View of the Obelisk Erected under Liberty-Tree in Boston on the Rejoicings for the Repeal of the — Stamp Act,* **1766** (restrike 1943) (detail). Engraving. Courtesy of the Library of Congress Prints and Photographs Division, LC-USZC4-4599

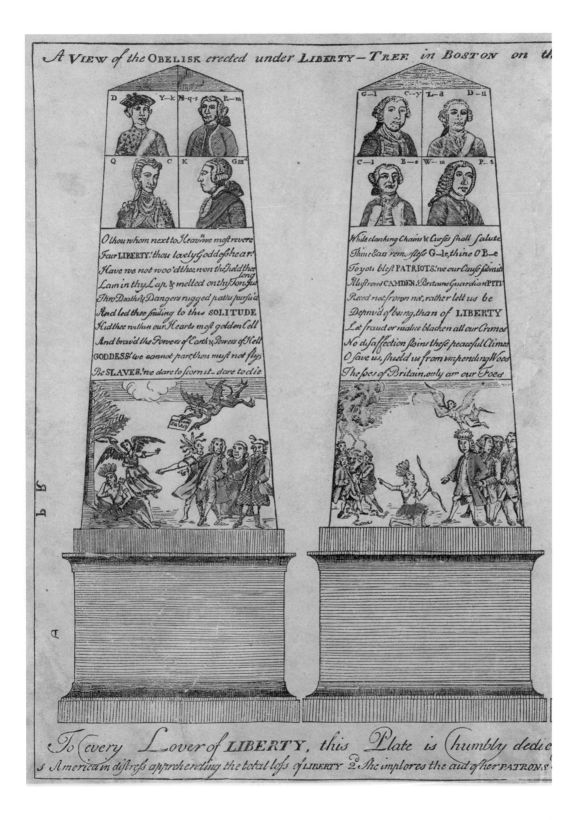

ALTHOUGH MORE THAN two hundred and fifty years had elapsed since the engraver Johann Froschauer had first depicted an indigenous American as a near-naked individual wearing a plumed skirt and stand-up feather headdress (see page 27), the figure had not lost any of its signifying power when it was taken over by the Sons of Liberty in the mid-1700s. On the contrary, members of the pre–Revolutionary War fraternal organization—American colonists who were defying the imposition of British taxes—deemed the readily available figure highly appropriate and charged it with deeply personal and political meaning. Around 1765, Great Britain began using the image of an Indian Princess to symbolize the mother-daughter relationship it imagined having with the colonies (Fleming 1965, 65; Olson 1991, 75–123). Ingeniously, the Sons of Liberty appropriated the sign not to represent a filial relationship but rather, to distinguish themselves from their adversaries, namely, members of the British Parliament, who were taxing the Crown's North American colonies (see page 46).

The print *Liberty Triumphant* of 1774 gives no hint that any form of reconciliation or continued political subordination is possible (Olson 1991, 113). Attributed to Henry Dawkins, an English-born engraver who was active in New York and Philadelphia, *Liberty Triumphant* is in fact one of the most charged political images of the late eighteenth century, particularly of the so-called Intolerable Acts of 1774. Lord North and the British ministry, who proposed a trade monopoly on the colonies, are depicted on the left. Above them, Britannia decries the "conduct of those my degenerate Sons." On the right, the Sons of Liberty—who have donned plumed skirts and feather headdresses and who are united in their defiance—are led by America, portrayed as an Indian woman wearing a long gown and a stand-up feather headdress. She has taken aim at the parliamentarians and is about to shoot an arrow from her bow directly at them. She urges the Sons of Liberty to "aid me, and prevent my being fetter'd." Above her, Britannia commends the courage of the sons to Fame, who vows to "trumpet their noble Deeds from Pole to Pole."

With this proto-American usage of the two-and-a-half-century-old sign of near-naked individuals wearing plumed skirts and stand-up feather headdresses (first employed by Froschauer in 1505 to portray coastal Brazilian Tupinambás), the image had attained the status of a moral value. The central figure, now garbed in a long, loosely fitting dress, embodied not only liberty from Britain but also the Enlightenment ideal of Liberty, with all that this political and philosophical concept entailed in the eighteenth century. The Sons of Liberty's appropriation of Britain's American Indian imagery to identify themselves and their cause would set in motion Americans' ongoing custom of using American Indian imagery to distinguish themselves from Europeans and personify their most cherished value, liberty. The association of American Indians with liberty would not only be picked up by subsequent American patriotic and fraternal societies (see pages 86 and 91) but also become an American mainstay.

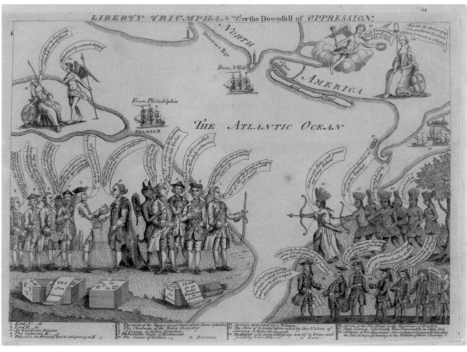

Attributed to Henry Dawkins (active ca. 1753–ca. 1786). *Liberty Triumphant: or the Downfall of Oppression,* **1774.** Etching. Courtesy of the John Carter Brown Library at Brown University, Providence, Rhode Island 31573

THE ROYAL AMERICAN MAGAZINE, *or Universal Repository of Instruction and Amusement* was a short lived but influential monthly periodical published in Boston from January 1774 to March 1775. Its articles addressed topics ranging from politics, medicine, and agriculture to literature, religion and advice for ladies. Its founding editor was Isaiah Thomas, a publisher well known for his strongly expressed political beliefs. Despite its title and the fact that it was published under the British provincial governor, it supported the cause of the American patriots who, since the Stamp Act was imposed in 1765, were becoming discontented with, and vocal about, various aspects of British rule in the thirteen colonies.

American patriots cut across all strata of society. Whether small-scale farmers or merchants, artisans, or wealthy and educated landowners, they were opposed to heavy taxes, lack of political representation and, more and more, the idea of the British occupying "their country." Tensions between patriots and the British, including their Loyalist supporters in the colonies, increasingly dominated public discourse in the 1760s and 1770s and spawned the tradition of American political prints (see pages 46 and 50).

During the eighteenth century, political prints were considered an effective weapon of criticism. In Britain, they were published in newspapers intended for large and diverse reading audiences and were an accepted part of social and political life. Their effectiveness rested on satire, which was often a purely visual assault lobbed against one's political opponents. No less a person than Benjamin Franklin is credited with creating the first political cartoon in the American colonies.

This vignette, which appeared on the title page of the first and most of the subsequent issues of the *Royal American Magazine,* may well be regarded as a political print. It is certainly satirical. Made by the ardent patriot Paul Revere, it represents two allegories. On the left is an Indian Princess, who represents the thirteen colonies, or Daughters of Britannia, and on the right is the Genius of Knowledge. In European art, allegories were long used to depict morals and other abstract concepts, such as time or charity, in addition to physical entities, such as the continents (see page 31). Later generations came to regard the allegories as "hidden meanings" in paintings and other forms of visual expression, but the figures were easily read in their day (Battistini 2005).

Following the way allegories of the "New World" were depicted in European map cartouches (see page 33), Revere placed his two allegories within an ornamental border. As a silversmith and furniture maker, Revere would have been aware of English fashions in decorative arts. Conforming to the English rococo, or Chippendale, style, his border typifies upper-class British artistic sensibilities of the second half of eighteenth century.

Inside the border and at the left sits the Indian Princess, or allegory of the Daughters of Britannia, a convention used in Britain between 1765 and 1783

Paul Revere (1735–1818). Vignette published on the title page of the *Royal American Magazine*, 1774. Woodcut. Courtesy of the American Antiquarian Society, Worcester, Massachusetts

(Fleming 1965, 65). Revere intentionally placed his Indian Princess in a natural setting. Gardens, arbors, vines, plants, herbs, fruits, and flowers were imbued with symbolism in European art (Impelluso [2003] 2004). Young women in enclosed gardens, for example, were associated with values such as goodness. Revere's Indian Princess is situated in the wilderness, but not to evoke Europeans' usual negative associations with the untamed natural world. Standing in front of the Indian Princess is the Genius of Knowledge (Brigham [1954] 1969, 209)—a woman in a long flowing robe holding a small vase in her right hand and pointing upwards with a finger of her left hand. Throughout the Enlightenment, Europeans were fascinated with human accomplishments and consumed by the quest for knowledge. *The Royal American Magazine* itself was dedicated to the art of reading and thus the pursuit of knowledge.

Revere's Indian Princess extends with her left hand a pipe known as a calumet, which has a stone bowl and a long wooden stem adorned with feathers. By including the calumet in the vignette, together with the bow and quiver full of arrows, Revere provided the Indian Princess with a new symbolic attribute, one imbued with deep meaning for American Indians. Calumets were a sacred badge of friendship and marked the solemnity of alliance-making occasions. Indian leaders often used them in the opening ceremonies of treaty meetings, and for calling upon the spirits of animals, especially birds. Today, they are most typically used on the northern plains and prairie. By the second half of the eighteenth century, however, delegations of American Indian leaders from farther inland were already traveling east on diplomatic missions. As the historian James Axtell has written, "Throughout much of eastern America in the seventeenth and eighteen centuries, the major vehicle for peaceful alliance was the calumet" (Axtell 2001, 27).

The calumet's meaning was not lost on American colonists. If Revere never witnessed a ceremony in which a Native leader used a calumet, he most certainly knew of them through publications in which they were illustrated, alongside accounts of meetings in which they were shared. Revere could have easily seen detailed illustrations of calumets and learned of their significance in books.[1]

Revere's vignette for the title page of the *Royal American Magazine* cleverly combined the eighteenth century's most potent visual motifs: a Chippendale border (a symbol of English refinement); the Indian Princess (Britain's personification of her daughters, the colonies); a classically garbed woman (a European personification of knowledge); and the calumet (to American Indians, one of the most profoundly important emblems of sincerity, diplomacy, and spirituality).

Colonial Americans were already appropriating Britain's image of the Indian Princess to represent themselves and symbolize their most cherished political virtue, liberty (see page 50). But in his title-page vignette for the *Royal American Magazine*, Revere expanded the iconographic repertoire for depicting *their* Indian Princess. Deliberately ensconced in the wilderness as a sign of defiance, she holds her ground against any British notions of superiority by offering her calumet with unaffected solemnity. Paul Revere, a highly skilled artisan and dedicated patriot, created an image that expressed the sentiments of patriots who had tired of British imperial rule in American life and government. No longer wanting to remain part of the Empire and its aristocratic trappings, they were advancing knowledge *in* America.

Francis Hopkinson (1737–1791). Design proposal for the Great Seal of the United States, 1780.
Record Group 360, Records of the Continental and Confederation Congresses 205 National Archives and Records Administration, Washington, DC

ON JULY 4, 1776, the Continental Congress formed a committee to create a design for what would become known as the Great Seal of the United States. The seal was to represent the sovereignty of the soon-to-be-independent United States of America, and it would be affixed to important national documents requiring authentication (Patterson and Dougall 1976, 2; U.S. Department of State 2003, 1). Dissatisfied with the first committee's design proposals, the Continental Congress formed a second committee in 1780. Like the first, the second committee was composed of learned and distinguished men with impeccable revolutionary credentials.[1] The panel turned to noted lawyer Francis Hopkinson to assist them. Hopkinson, who in 1776 had signed the Declaration of Independence as a member of the Continental Congress, was artistically inclined and had a deep interest in heraldry. He had facilitated the design of New Jersey's state seal in 1776, purportedly designed the first official American flag in 1777, and would design the original Orrery Seal of the University of Pennsylvania in 1782 (University of Pennsylvania, 2016).

The first design that Hopkinson proposed for the Great Seal incorporates an image of an American Indian man and a female figure. The two figures flank and support a shield bearing fifteen stripes. A constellation of thirteen six-pointed stars hovering above the scene represents the thirteen states.

The woman wears a diaphanous dress and olive-branch crown and holds an olive branch in one hand. She symbolizes peace. The American Indian figure is no less emblematic. Representing war, he is almost nude, with a robe draped over one shoulder. He has a distinctive indigenous hairstyle: both sides of the head are shaved, leaving a strip of hair on top of the head. He holds a bow and arrows in one hand and carries a quiver of arrows over his right shoulder. While the attributes of the female figure harken back to classical antiquity, those of the Indian man recall Europeans' earliest depictions of American Indians. Except for his hairstyle, well-known to colonial and first-generation Americans, he was no more dressed in contemporaneous garb than was the woman. Both figures were personifications. The motto on the ribbon below them reads: *Bello vel pace paratus* (Prepared in war or in peace).

In all, it took six years and three committees to arrive at the winning proposal for the Great Seal of the United States. While the motto changed to *E pluribus unum* (Out of many, one), the symbolic references to war and peace remained. In the final design an eagle holds an olive wreath in one talon and a bundle of thirteen arrows in the other. Together the olive branch and arrows "denote the power of peace and war," which is exclusively vested in Congress (U.S. Department of State 2003, 15).

Amazingly little scholarly attention has been paid to the incorporation of an American Indian as a prominent compositional element of the first proposal (Hunt 1909; Patterson and Dougall 1976; U.S. Department of State 2003). The reasons are perhaps various: one, Hopkinson himself reworked his first proposal and replaced the American Indian with a soldier holding a sword; two, the image of the soldier was dropped from later proposals; and, three, several of Hopkinson's original design elements, such as the striped shield and constellation of stars, were carried forward into the final design and are often noted. Still, that an image of an American Indian was seriously contemplated for the Great Seal of the United States is significant. It was included at the very moment the nascent United States was trying to define its form of government, codify its foundational ideas, and create a distinctive national identity.

Francis Hopkinson (1737–1791). Design proposal for the Great Seal of the United States, 1780 (detail). Record Group 360, Records of the Continental and Confederation Congresses 205 National Archives and Records Administration, Washington, DC

In 1761, four years after his graduation from the College of Philadelphia (now the University of Pennsylvania), Hopkinson had become the secretary of the Pennsylvania Indian Commission (Reynolds 1961, 1075). As such, he witnessed firsthand the central role American Indians played in British and colonial American economy and diplomacy. Equally important, the prominence of the American Indian in Hopkinson's first design for the Great Seal in 1780 suggests that the first generation of Americans, including a signer of the Declaration of Independence, acknowledged that the democratic country they were trying to create and hold together was on land carved out of indigenous North America. The borders of the United States that Great Britain and the United States would agree upon in 1783 with the signing of the Treaty of Paris were drawn around the territories of numerous Native nations. Many of those lands were still vast. Virtually all early maps of the United States identify the immense territories of powerful Native nations, and many of the maps depict American Indians within their cartouches (see page 58). In 1780 when Hopkinson drew his first design proposal, the United States and American Indians remained linked in the minds of Americans and Europeans.

Hopkinson's composition of an American Indian man and classically dressed woman flanking a shield beneath a constellation representing the thirteen states seems to suggest that the establishment of the United States might require an accommodation between Americans and American Indians. That Hopkinson proposed such a design for the Great Seal captures an important occasion in U.S. history. His removal of the American Indian from his second proposal seems almost to prefigure the U.S. Congress's passage in 1830 of the Indian Removal Act, which resulted in the removal of virtually all American Indians from within the settled borders of the United States (certainly its southern states). Fifty years after Hopkinson made his first attempt to codify the United States' foundational ideas in the Great Seal, the federal government pursued a policy of erasure that was symbolically prefigured by Hopkinson's reworking of his first proposal.

THE LARGE AND RICHLY DETAILED ENGLISH MAP of North America and the West Indies, created immediately after the signing of the Treaty of Paris of 1783, is one of the first European maps that attempts to show the boundaries of the new and independent United States. Specifically, it documents the land the treaty allocated to the United States. With the treaty's signing, the American Revolutionary War was formally ended and Great Britain recognized the sovereignty of its thirteen former colonies. The map illustrates the boundary between the newly independent nation and Great Britain's remaining colonies to the north.

More than that, the mapmakers undertook to document the most recent information concerning the geography and political landscape of all North America. They based this map on one made around 1775 that had already been revised several times to expand European knowledge of the continent (Stevens and Tree 1951, 337–9). The revision of 1783 presents California as part of the continent rather than the island shown on earlier maps. It locates the Mississippi and Missouri Rivers and identifies the Canadian Arctic. One inset illustrates Baffin and Hudson Bays, while another shows the mouth of the Colorado River, describing its "discovery" by Italian Jesuit missionary-explorer Eusebio Kino. The map identifies Spanish, French, British, and American possessions, including forts and roads as well as American Indian territories.

With an elaborately engraved cartouche, the map, intended for use on a wall, was printed on four pages and bound into the most important atlas of the era. It is noteworthy that as the world was continuing to expand its knowledge of North America—and beginning to recognize the United States geographically—Europeans were cartographically defining the continent and the new nation as they always had defined the "New World" and British American colonies: with images of American Indians as the primary symbols in its cartouches.

The designers of the 1783 map's cartouche made it virtually the same size as the United States. Like the earlier one upon which it is based, this map presents in its cartouche two prominently placed American Indians, comfortably surrounded by animals, including a parrot and a monkey, and what appears to be the hide of a wild cat—symbolizing both exoticism and North America. A cherub-like African child between them innocuously alludes to slavery. The Indian at left has an arm draped over the cartouche scrollwork, while the muscular figure at right appears equally at ease and fully outside the cartouche's scrollwork. In sharp contrast to the cartouche on the 1696 French map *Amerique septentrionale divisée en ses principales parties* (see page 33), these Indians are not enmeshed in the cartouche. Rather, they appear to possess it.

When the map was created in 1783, American Indians were decisive players in the geopolitics of North America. British commerce and diplomacy during the second half of the eighteenth century was hugely dependent on trade and alliances with its

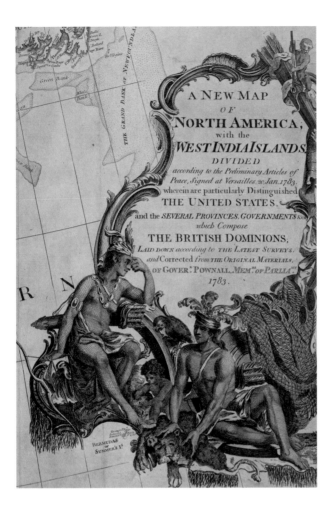

Thomas Pownall (1722–1805). *A new map of North America with the West India Islands: divided according to the preliminary articles of peace, signed at Versailles, 20, Jan. 1783;* wherein are particularly distinguished the United States and the several provinces, governments & ca. which compose the British dominions, 1783 (detail). Engraving. Published by Robert Sayer and John Bennett. Courtesy of the Lionel Pincus and Princess Firyal Map Division of the New York Public Library

colonies, which included American Indians. Although American Indians were not present at the signing of the Treaty of Paris and it was signed "without so much as a mention of the tribes" (Calloway 1999, 23), European empires saw them as real political and military powers.

At that time the United States was, relatively speaking, a weak national power. It was not until after the United States ratified its constitution in 1788 that the newly independent nation established internal boundaries between states and confirmed states' western boundaries (Library of Congress 2013). Although Native nations suffered from and were severely disrupted by the Revolutionary War, "Indians remained a force to be reckoned with during and after the revolution," as one historian wrote (Horsman 1999, 23). Most American Indian nations allied with the British during the war, while some sided with the colonial rebels. The fledgling United States would have to come to terms with all the Native nations—whose

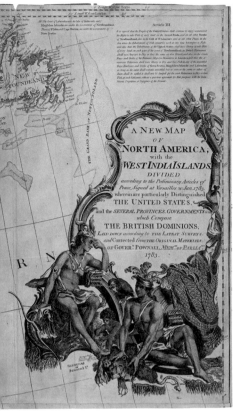

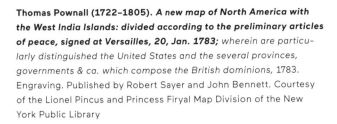

Thomas Pownall (1722–1805). *A new map of North America with the West India Islands: divided according to the preliminary articles of peace, signed at Versailles, 20, Jan. 1783;* wherein are particularly distinguished the United States and the several provinces, governments & ca. which compose the British dominions, 1783. Engraving. Published by Robert Sayer and John Bennett. Courtesy of the Lionel Pincus and Princess Firyal Map Division of the New York Public Library

lands its citizens now coveted. Americans would have to either go to war (again) or negotiate for land acquisitions, trade, and peaceful relations. The new nation-state could not ignore but rather, had to contend with, American Indians, who remained a political, economic, military, and cultural presence (Calloway 1999, 23). In many profound ways, American Indians would define the history of the emerging American republic.

It is interesting to note that the cartouche on the first map compiled, printed, and published in the United States is also rich in symbolism of the new nation (primary symbols in its cartouche include the newly designed American flag and an American woman holding a liberty pole). The map was published in 1784 by an engraver named Abel Buell. But it is the cartouche on the English map of 1783, created immediately after the signing of the Treaty of Paris, that more accurately evokes the political landscape of North America.

DANIEL MORGAN

(1736–1802) was an untutored teenage runaway and contentious New Jersey–born Virginian—in short, a frontiersman—who fought during the French and Indian War and then the Revolutionary War, ultimately achieving the rank of brigadier general. On March 25, 1790, he was presented with a Congressional Gold Medal in recognition of his victory in a pivotal battle during the war for independence.[1] In that encounter, Morgan, then a colonel, distinguished himself as a master tactician by defeating one of the most hated British officers of the war. On the morning of January 17, 1781, Morgan and British Lieutenant Colonel Banastre Tarleton met in a backwoods pastureland in present-day South Carolina for what became known as the Battle of Cowpens.

Based on his tactical genius and innate ability to read the terrain, Morgan devised a plan that provoked a premature charge by Tarleton and the troops under Tarleton's command (Babits 2001, 152). They were lured directly into a trap. In less than an hour Morgan's force mortally wounded 110 British soldiers and captured 830 more. It also commandeered Tarleton's supplies and equipment. The Battle of Cowpens was the precursor to the Battle of Yorktown, the final conflict of the war. For this reason Morgan was credited with paving the way for British surrender and American independence (ibid., 1).

Congress adopted the practice of awarding gold medals during the Revolutionary War (Glassman 2017, 1). George Washington, commander of the Continental Army, was the first to be so honored. General Morgan was one of only six others to receive a Congressional Gold Medal for service during the American Revolution. The reverse side of Morgan's medal depicts the then colonel making his victorious stand against Tarleton and his men. The front presents an allegorical Indian Queen, symbolizing the United States, crowning Morgan with a laurel wreath; his hand rests upon his sword. By the war's end, the Indian Princess who had represented the thirteen British American colonies as Daughters of Britannia now appeared as the Indian Queen, whom Americans fully embraced as a symbol for the United States. She now graphically distinguished Americans as a people distinct from Europeans; Americans were a different sort of being, one born out of the fight for liberty.

The queen on Morgan's medal differs from earlier representations of the Indian Princess, most notably in her decidedly classical stance, a contrapposto pose in which her body is elegantly twisted and her weight rests on one leg. The stance is a stylistic convention that can be traced to imagery on official objects used by Virginia's colonial government (Olson 1991, 232), including regimental flags. Interestingly, Virginia's version of the figure is often shown wearing a skirt of tobacco leaves, the colony's foundational cash crop.

The iconography on Morgan's congressional medal was meant not only to pay tribute to him (he was twice honored, as the recipient of the laurel wreath and the medal itself) but also to express the United States' ideas about itself as a new republic. It was intended to evoke ancient Rome and signal that the United States was a "republic under construction on the American continent" (Olson 1991, 233).

Americans were no longer appropriating British imagery to represent the colonies (see pages 46 and 50); they were employing a new pictorial language. Lester C. Olson, a scholar of early American emblems, observed that this new pictorial language emerged after the outbreak of the Revolutionary War, after which "imagery of a British heritage" had become unacceptable to Americans (Olson 1991, 234). He suggests that Americans felt an affinity with American Indians in the sense that they regarded themselves as being like American Indians: a "new race" forged out of the Revolutionary War, after which the Indian Princess motif was reconstituted with classical, or stately, attributes fitting a new republic.

THOMAS JEFFERSON conceived the United States' diplomatic medal *To Peace and Commerce* in 1792. Jefferson, then secretary of state, wanted the United States to present departing foreign dignitaries with a gift that symbolized the country's appreciation for their service in fostering shared peace and mutual prosperity. Readily approved by President George Washington, the medal's design underscores the importance Jefferson and the president placed on "developing commercial ties with Europe—without becoming embroiled in European conflicts" (U.S. Department of State 2016).

The oldest official visual representation of the United States—that is, made by the government of the United States—is an American Indian. The image of the Indian Queen had been employed a few years earlier on Congressional Gold Medals presented to Revolutionary War heroes (Fleming 1965, 39). The diplomatic medal made in 1792 is one of the first instances in which the United States formally created an allegory of itself and presented it to a foreign nation. In doing so, the United States again represented itself as an Indian Queen.

Thomas Jefferson, who is credited with the medal's basic design, did not consider American artisans up to the task and recommended that it be made by one of two highly respected French artists. The great French sculptor and engraver Augustin Dupré was Jefferson's first choice. Dupré received the commission and created the die for the medal; two gold and eight bronze medals were struck from it.

Unlike Paul Revere's Indian Princess, who was created for political prints, the Indian Queen on the front of this diplomatic medal (as on Congressional Gold

Medals) is decidedly classical in terms of her anatomical proportions, including her face and pose. Indeed, the entire treatment of her figure complements that of the contrapposto figure of Mercury, the Roman god of science and commerce, who stands before her. The allegory of America as an American Indian is unambiguously represented by her feather headdress, quiver, and feather skirt. Half cloaked, she is regally seated next to several large crates tied for shipment, a barrel, and an anchor. She holds out a cornucopia, welcoming Mercury to her shore. Standing to her right, Mercury holds a caduceus, or short staff encircled by snakes. Behind him, in the distance, is a U.S. merchant vessel representing commerce with Europe. The reverse of the medal (shown at right) is engraved with the Great Seal of the United States.

By representing America symbolically as an American Indian and linking that image with those of commerce, Jefferson's peace and commerce medal is as disquieting as it is handsome. The medal encapsulates the idea that republicanism and progress would be built on trade. Jefferson's ambition "to master a continent" (Meacham 2013, 410) has most often been linked with his vision of a yeoman republic, but he had another goal to which the medal speaks. Jefferson was calling for a commercial as well as a territorial empire.

It was of no concern to Jefferson that North America's indigenous peoples were key players in Atlantic trade networks; the medal's Indian Queen does not represent American Indians. She represents the land, specifically the abundance it could provide and the wealth that could be extracted from it. Jefferson's notion of advancing the good of the country—of building an Empire of Liberty—was predicated on acquiring indigenous lands and promoting free trade. The medal speaks not of a relationship with Indians but of a newly formed republic with a global commercial mission. As the United States' peace and commerce medal attests, the symbolic usurpation of the Indian Princess image had been accomplished. The concrete usurpation of American Indian land would follow.

Joseph Richardson Jr. (1752–1831). George Washington peace medal, 1792. Stamped silver. National Museum of the American Indian, Smithsonian Institution 22/8915

THE OUTWARDLY SIMPLE BUT ENDURING IMAGE of a nearly naked man or woman wearing a plumed skirt and stand-up feather headdress—signifying first the entire "New World" and its indigenous peoples and then, more specifically, colonial America and the North American Indians inhabiting it—found one of its final incarnations on a George Washington peace medal made in 1792. After the Revolutionary War, Americans swiftly had to come to terms with how Enlightenment principals concerning the nature and rights of man applied to American Indians. Henry Knox, President Washington's secretary of war from 1789 to 1794, outlined the United States' first carefully reasoned Indian policy (Horsman 1999, 39). Like many early American political thinkers, Knox was not only deeply influenced by the new intellectual and political ideas of what we now call Enlightenment but also troubled by how U.S. government interactions with American Indians would affect European perceptions of American democracy. Knox argued that it would be a "stain on the character of the nation" to dispossess Indians of their land by force (quoted in Horsman 1999, 43). He made three proposals: that the United States respect the primacy of American Indians and their boundaries, that negotiations with American Indians be centralized under the federal government, and that the federal government have the sole right to enter into treaties with Indians. In accord with Knox, President Washington throughout his presidency personally negotiated treaties between the newly formed United States and American Indian nations within its borders. He also initiated the practice of presenting to Indian leaders a medal bearing an image of the president, signifying his role as head of state. This George Washington peace medal represents an important historical moment—the beginning of the United States' formal interactions with American Indians inside its national borders.

Significantly, the Indian depicted on one side of the medal looks nothing like the Indian Queen figure on the nearly contemporaneous Congressional Gold Medal presented to Brigadier General Daniel Morgan and on the U.S. peace and commerce medal. Here the Indian figure wears a crescent-shaped silver gorget, a diplomatic gift he would have received from either a European power or the United States. The gorget intentionally and unambiguously identifies him as a Native leader. He and the president extend hands, while the Indian leader's tomahawk has been dropped to the ground. Both gestures are important signs of peace. Even more symbolically charged is the positioning of the Indian leader and president before several cultivated fields and an American farmer plowing with two oxen. The Indian figure contrasts markedly with the tilled fields behind him. The scene plainly associates farming with American—as opposed to American Indian—societies, even though American Indians throughout what had become the thirteen states extensively cultivated corn, beans, squash, and other crops.

That a centuries-old tradition for representing American Indians was used on the George Washington peace medal is no accident. The figure of the Native leader is clearly intended to imply a lack of farming knowledge. His plumed skirt and stand-up feather headdress are not the garb worn by any Indian person, let alone a Native leader, whom George Washington would have encountered. The image evokes the notion that Indians (writ large) are wanderers who neither live in settled villages nor grow crops and, consequently, do not use the land productively. That Washington presented such medals to Native leaders, and insisted that only the president of the United States negotiate with Indians for land, implies that acquiring "vast tracts of unsettled territories within the boundaries of the United States" (Alexander Hamilton 1797, quoted in Scigliano 2001, 34) was a national interest—and that transforming those tracts into orderly agricultural plots was foundational to the United States.

This potent image, however, with the addition of the gorget, also unequivocally suggests that to acquire land (i.e., to expand its foothold on the continent), the United States would have to deal with American Indians and their leaders. It signifies the reality (however unwanted it may have been) that American and American Indian lives were and would remain historically, geographically, and politically interwoven. The Indian image, together with that of George Washington, engraved on this peace medal expresses the attitude, if not dominant moral judgment, that the U.S. government, to establish its legitimacy, must respect the political authority of Native nations. For Knox and Washington, the federal government needed to assert its authority over states that were seeking to negotiate with Native nations. Equally important, the federal government had to demonstrate the workings of U.S. democracy under the watchful eyes of Europeans.

NICHOLAS GEVELOT'S SANDSTONE RELIEF *William Penn's Treaty with the Indians* is one of four installed over the doorways leading into the rotunda of the Capitol of the United States.[1] The Capitol was built not only to house the legislative branch of the United States government but also to be a "symbol of American democracy and liberty" (Kennon and Somma 2004, 59). As a tribute to and in emulation of the Roman republic, the large ceremonial rotunda was designed to evoke the ancient Roman Pantheon. While the rotunda's classical design and references throughout the building are unmistakable, most of the artwork in the chamber, including Gevelot's relief, is devoted to colonial and early American history. Gevelot was a French-born sculptor trained in Italy.

Europe (England and France, at any rate) had extolled William Penn's negotiations with Lenape Indians for land in 1682, long before the United States was established. With the founding of the republic, those negotiations were quickly adopted and celebrated as one of the country's foundational events. Fittingly, all the iconographic elements in Gevelot's relief symbolize harmonious coexistence: the two cooing birds in an elm tree; the Lenape man's pipe; the scroll Penn holds, with its unmissable inscription, "Treaty 1682"; and above all the handshake (Fryd 2001, 30–31).

In 1682, Penn, a leader in the English Quaker Society of Friends, immigrated to the British American colonies with his congregation and founded the Province of Pennsylvania. He wanted to found a "holy experiment" in America, that is, a colony based on principles of justice, where religious and civic freedom would be guaranteed to all. Europeans applauded his interactions with the Lenape for two reasons: first, in the view of the English, Penn did not need to offer to pay the Lenape for land the English king had granted him, but he did so anyway, out of principle. Second, Penn's negotiations with the Lenape were friendly, respectful, and peaceful—in other words, fully consistent with his professed values. Penn's exemplary relationship with the Lenape was regarded so highly that the French Enlightenment philosopher Voltaire discussed it in his English-language *Letters Concerning the English Nation* (1733), which was published in French the following year as *Lettres philosophiques* (Voltaire [1733] 2007, 1–14). Voltaire saw larger forces at work in Penn's actions vis-à-vis the integration of Europeans and indigenous peoples in the "New World." He recognized that European expansion was largely harmful to indigenous peoples (ibid., 11–14) and argued that the only way to engage indigenous peoples was to abide by certain notions of what we now regard as human rights.

There is no reason not to believe that Penn wanted his fellow Quaker colonists "to live soberly and kindly together" with the Lenape Indians, as he did. But by 1682, Quaker immigration had exploded. In that year twenty-three ships—filled with two thousand emigrants—sailed into Delaware Bay. One of the ships was the *Welcome*, which carried Penn—and smallpox (Fischer 1989, 421). Between 1682

Nicholas Gevelot (active 1820s– 1850s). *William Penn's Treaty with the Indians, 1682,* **1827.** Sandstone. U.S. Capitol rotunda, Washington, DC. Courtesy of the Architect of the Capitol

and 1685, ninety more shiploads of Quakers arrived, and it has been estimated that twenty-three thousand Quakers settled in the Delaware Valley between 1675 and 1715 (ibid.). After 1750, the number of Quakers doubled in every generation.

The onslaught of colonists and their relentless desire for more land had a devastating effect on the Lenape people—it threatened their very survival. After Penn's death, his sons took charge of Pennsylvania. They did not share their father's ideals, nor did they recognize the compact the elder Penn had made with the Lenape. As a result the Lenape were driven to the Susquehanna Valley, then into Ohio. In the nineteenth century, they were forced to move west several more times. By the time Penn's diplomatic accomplishment was enshrined in the U.S. Capitol rotunda, Penn's sons and subsequent generations of Quakers had rendered his actions virtually meaningless.

The relief Gevelot made in 1827, thought to have been based upon the Silvanus Bevan William Penn Medal of 1720, further cemented a narrative of peace and friendship between the Quakers and Lenape, making no reference to the calamitous events that followed the famed negotiations (Fryd 2001, 30). Just nine years later, in 1836, an organization calling itself the Society for the Commemoration of the Landing of William Penn charged that since the days of Penn, "aggressors enlightened by science, ennobled by Christianity, carried on a series of exterminating wars, killing, defrauding and dispossessing" American Indians (Tyson 1836, 15). But, wittingly or not on Gevelot's part, his relief masked the ruinous impact of colonialism on American Indians both in the 1600s, when the depicted event occurred, and in the 1800s, when Gevelot created the work.

Gevelot's relief, as it turned out, was severely criticized in its day. It was considered "heavy and dull in its execution" (Kennon and Somma 2004, 69) and falling short of capturing Penn's virtues. It is unlikely, however, that the Society for the Commemoration of the Landing of William Penn was much concerned with Gevelot's artistic execution. They were preoccupied with imploring the government to extend Penn's virtues of friendship and justice to Cherokees, who were being pressured to leave their ancestral homelands, first by the state of Georgia and then by means of a fraudulent treaty (Tyson 1836, 3).

John Gadsby Chapman (1808–1889). *Baptism of Pocahontas,* **1839.** Oil on canvas. U.S. Capitol rotunda, Washington, DC. Courtesy of the Architect of the Capitol

AMERICAN PAINTER JOHN GADSBY CHAPMAN'S *Baptism of Pocahontas* was commissioned as one of a series of eight immense oil paintings of historical events for the rotunda of the Capitol of the United States. The paintings are installed on the curved walls underneath the rotunda's majestic dome and below a monochromatic band of frescoes known as the *Frieze of American History*. Each painting is presented in an opulent gilded frame and depicts an epic event in either colonial or U.S. history. Essentially a hymn in praise of conquest, *Baptism of Pocahontas* portrays both, insofar as European as well as American success in North America was perceived to have begun with Pocahontas.

Although historians today largely dismiss the story as fiction, Pocahontas (ca. 1595–1617), the daughter of the Powhatan Confederacy's leader, had long been credited with saving the life in 1607 of English colonist Captain John Smith and, by extension, the Jamestown colony and the Virginia Company of London.[1]

71

John Gadsby Chapman (1808–1889). *Baptism of Pocahontas,* **1839** (detail). Oil on canvas. U.S. Capitol rotunda, Washington, DC. Courtesy of the Architect of the Capitol

The Virginia Company was a pioneer capitalist venture in the "New World," a joint-stock company chartered by the British Crown. The company backed the Jamestown colonists; its interests were in establishing a commercial, rather than a territorial, empire. Their profit was to be extracted from the New World. That wealth turned out to be an extremely lucrative cash crop: tobacco (see page 40). For these reasons, Pocahontas's supposed rescue of John Smith from imminent death was considered instrumental in making Virginia the first successful colony in the British Empire as well as, later, the wealthiest and most influential state in the newly established United States.

Chapman's *Baptism of Pocahontas* is executed in the grand tradition of Western historical and religious painting. From the Renaissance through the second half of the nineteenth century, an artist's most prestigious paintings almost always dealt with at least one of three themes: historical subject matter, religious events, or Greek and Roman mythology. Chapman's painting achieved two of these. On the surface, it portrays British and, by extension, American success in instilling in American Indians the doctrines and practices of Christianity. The painting also illustrates Pocahontas's baptism as a powerfully symbolic act, which Britain and, later, the United States believed signaled their triumph over Native North America.

Pocahontas was at the center of many dramatic events during a momentous historical period. Yet, as significant as Pocahontas's baptism was to the English and early Americans, and as carefully as Chapman researched the event (he traveled through America and to England to study period churches), it took place neither in such exalted surroundings nor under such lofty circumstances as Chapman imagined. English colonists at James Fort abducted Pocahontas and held her captive for a year, first at Jamestown and then at Henricus (the English settlement established in 1611). There Reverend Alexander Whitaker gave her religious instruction and, in 1614, baptized her. Shortly afterward, Pocahontas married colonist John Rolfe in a rustic chapel at James Fort.

In Chapman's portrayal, Pocahontas is surrounded by a large English congregation, including husband-to-be John Rolfe, the Reverend Whitaker, and the governor of James Fort (Fryd 2001, 147). Few of her Powhatan relatives are present. Seated on the right is her uncle, who expresses his displeasure with the ceremony by frowning and turning away. He is presented as a foil to emphasize the boldness of Pocahontas's conversion and fervor of her devoutness. While the dramatic events in her short life have been documented, there is no historical record of what she thought about her abduction, religious indoctrination, baptism, or even marriage. During the past four hundred years, many have conjectured Pocahontas's true beliefs.

During the first decades of the nascent United States, Henry Knox, a close friend and adviser to George Washington and the first American charged with formulating a national policy toward Indians, developed the idea that intermarriage might be a means of assimilating American Indians into American society (Horsman 1991, 39). Knox was not alone in his belief concerning the potential of intermarriage. Thomas Jefferson also entertained the notion (ibid., 50). Believing that Indians "should be inculcated into the ways of whites" (Meacham 2013, 111), Jefferson told a delegation of Lenape (Delaware), Mohican, and Munsee in December 1808 "You will unite yourselves with us, and we shall all be Americans. You will mix with us by marriage. Your blood will run in our veins and will spread with us over this great island" (quoted in Horsman 1991, 50).

Jefferson's own daughter, Martha, married into the prestigious Randolph family, which was descended from Pocahontas and John Rolfe. Martha and Thomas Randolph's second son, a direct descendant of Pocahontas, was the first child born in the President's House (later called the White House) (Kierner 2012, 77). Jefferson was far from being the only prominent early American with Indian ancestry in his family. Many of Virginia's elite, known as the First Families of Virginia, have long touted their Native lineage, including their descent from Pocahontas.

Nonetheless, by 1840, when *Baptism of Pocahontas* was installed in the Capitol rotunda, in effect making Pocahontas a high priestess in the country's civic temple, the country had abandoned its fanciful marriage strategy for "civilizing" American Indians. Ten years earlier, the federal government initiated its first great assertion of power over American Indians by signing into law the Indian Removal Act. Marshalling its entire bureaucratic apparatus, the government in 1830 began the process of removing Southeast Indian nations from territories east of the Mississippi River.

As the United States was implementing this bold political initiative, Pocahontas was officially received into the pantheon of honored ancestors and acknowledged as a founder of the country. She is the only Native woman so exalted in the Capitol rotunda—by a nation that had little interest in establishing strong cultural and political contacts with contemporary American Indian societies but rather, concentrated on gaining control of their land.[2]

IN 1846, CONGRESS COMMISSIONED Henry Rowe Schoolcraft (1793–1864) to conduct a major study of American Indians tribes. Schoolcraft was an explorer, geologist, glass manufacturer, Indian agent, author, and an early figure in the history of anthropological inquiry who sought to influence U.S. policy concerning American Indians. His study took ten years and resulted in a six-volume work titled *Historical and Statistical Information Respecting the History, Condition, and Prospects of the Indian Tribes of the United States*. As printed on its title page, the work was prepared under the direction of the Bureau of Indian Affairs per an act of Congress on March 30, 1847, and was published by the authority of Congress. The cover of each of the six volumes was embossed and gilded with the same dramatic image of an American Indian. The artist of the vivid scene based it on a watercolor drawing by Seth Eastman, an artist and U.S. Army captain (see page 94). Several years after painting the watercolor, Eastman made an oil painting of the same scene, titled *The Death Whoop* (1868). The painting hung in the U.S. Capitol's House Indian Affairs Committee room until 1987 (Fryd 2001, 173–74).

The image Eastman created and re-created, which is embossed on each volume of Schoolcraft's work, is an archetype—not of the noble savage, the vanishing Indian, or the Indian Princess but rather, of the murderous savage who is impervious to moral teachings and removed from the possibility of salvation. The Indian stands over a prone white man, holding the victim's scalp in one hand and a knife in the other. The portrayal represents the worst of all possible encounters between an American and an Indian—between the civilized and the savage. Visually exact in its details and meaning, the image was an apt choice; as a scholar of American literature, Roy Harvey Pearce, observed, "The idea of savagism culminated in the work of Henry Rowe Schoolcraft" (Pearce 1965, 120).

Following the thinking of European and American social theorists of the day, Schoolcraft was a monogenist—a proponent of a social evolutionary theory that all mankind advanced through stages of savagery, barbarism, and civilization, and that these stages could be reflected in a society's technology, kinship, form of government, and attitudes toward property (Bieder 1986, 156). Based on this type of thinking, Americans categorized American Indians as savages—usually meaning that their "race," at home in the depths of the wilderness, had not yet attained civilization and, more damning still, was far from achieving it. Indians were at a standstill, unresponsive to the march of time and the laws of the universe. Schoolcraft was increasingly dogmatic about what he saw as American Indians' inability to accept Christianity (Bieder 1986, 162).

Despite his belief that American Indians were incapable of advancing themselves and becoming civilized, Schoolcraft felt it was important that the United States study its "free, bold, wild, independent, Native race" (quoted in Hinsley 1981, 20). He proposed (curiously) that the history of American Indians was the

Unknown artist after watercolor by Seth Eastman (1808–1875). *The Death Whoop*, 1849–55. Cover of Henry Rowe Schoolcraft's *Historical and Statistical Information Respecting the History, Condition, and Prospects of the Indian Tribes of the United States,* vols. 1–6, 1851–57. Courtesy of Smithsonian Institution Libraries, Washington, DC, Joseph F. Cullman 3rd Library of Natural History

history of Americans, and that Americans were obliged to preserve their collective memory of the "red man." In 1836, Schoolcraft was promoted to the office of Michigan's Superintendent of Indian Affairs. During this time, he married the daughter of an Irish fur trader and an Ojibwe woman, and during a period of thirty years carried out the ethnographic work for which he is best known and in some ways appreciated: his compilations of Ojibwe songs, oratory, and oral narratives.[1]

Schoolcraft's and other monogenists' thinking about American Indians dismantled and then reconstructed Enlightenment thought about human nature and the rights of man. Schoolcraft asserted that his theories about Indians were based upon close observation that allowed him to perceive what American Indians thought, felt, and desired—in other words, what was most fundamental about them. But he thought that American Indians had degenerated since the time of Noah and had slid backward on the scale of mankind (Bieder 1986, 177). His assertions were not based on any genuine understanding of American Indians or, for that matter, science.

A self-professed expert in the "mental characteristics" of American Indians, Schoolcraft openly advocated for their removal so that they could become "rehabilitated" and, not coincidentally, land could be freed up for Euro-American settlement. Schoolcraft himself concluded treaties in which the Ottawa and Ojibwe ceded millions of acres of land in Michigan Territory to the United States (Kappler 1903, 334–39 and 342–43).

Schoolcraft's work has been described by the early-twentieth-century anthropologist A. Irving Hallowell as a "ponderous hodge-podge of material in . . . six huge volumes" (1946, 142). It was not even well received in its day (Frankel 2000, 492). The project had grown out of Schoolcraft's proposal in September 1846 to the board of regents of the newly established Smithsonian Institution, titled "Plan for the Investigation of American Ethnology." Representing the dominant thinking about American Indians during the mid-nineteenth century, it resulted in the handsomely produced six volumes, each gilded with an ingenious Indian archetype that instilled fear with immense clarity and helped provide justification for the U.S. government's continuance of its removal policies. The Eastman/Schoolcraft gilded archetype of a murderous savage encapsulates the intersection of nineteenth-century "science" and federal Indian policy.

Unknown artist after watercolor by Seth Eastman (1808–1875). ***The Death Whoop,*** **1849–55.** Cover of Henry Rowe Schoolcraft's *Historical and Statistical Information Respecting the History, Condition, and Prospects of the Indian Tribes of the United States,* vols. 1–6, 1851–57 (detail). Courtesy of Smithsonian Institution Libraries, Washington, DC, Joseph F. Cullman 3rd Library of Natural History

THE THREE-DOLLAR GOLD COINS issued by the U.S. Mint from 1854 to 1889 bear an image of Liberty wearing an American Indian feather headdress with a headband labeled with her name. In Europe, the philosophical concept of liberty, meaning the social and political freedom of citizens, had long been presented allegorically as a woman. This practice dates to classical antiquity. The Roman goddess Libertas, for example, was depicted on ancient Roman coins in profile and wearing a crown. The notion of freedom was, of course, central to Americans, whose new government was firmly based on Enlightenment ideas and whose constitution guaranteed liberty for all citizens. Not surprisingly, then, female personifications of liberty have been on U.S. coins since 1793, when Liberty appeared on a copper half-cent coin. On that coin, she is depicted bareheaded, but she carries a soft cap, widely known as a liberty cap, mounted on a pole. The liberty cap and the cap mounted on a pole figure prominently in early American patriotic illustrations, even those dating to before the American Revolution (see page 46). Worn by formerly enslaved people in ancient Rome, the (usually red) cap was adopted as the symbol of liberty or freedom during the American and French Revolutions. Depictions of Liberty on U.S. coins have varied widely, with the greatest difference being what Liberty is shown wearing (or not) on her head; over the years, the increasing tendency was to represent her as a Greek or Roman goddess.

In 1858, James B. Longacre, who was chief engraver for the U.S. Bureau of the Mint and the designer of the three-dollar gold coin, explained in a letter that he had been reluctant to use on the coin a Greek or Roman symbol as an emblem of U.S. national identity. Longacre thought it far more appropriate to select a distinctively American symbol, and he chose to depict Liberty wearing the feather headdress "worn by American Indians throughout the hemisphere." He wrote, "Why should we in seeking a type for the illustration or symbol of a nation that need not hold itself lower than the Roman virtue or the Science of Greece prefer the barbaric period of a remote and distant people, from which to draw an emblem of nationality: to the aboriginal period of our own land: especially when the latter presents us with a characteristic distinction not less interesting, and more peculiar, than that which still casts its chain over the civilized portion of the older continent?" (Taxay 1966, 214). Interestingly, Longacre was criticized in some quarters for conflating Liberty with an American Indian. Evidently some of his compatriots did not recall that the Indian Princess had become a standard emblem of the American colonies in second half of the eighteenth century (Fleming 1965, 70) and, further, that Thomas Jefferson and Congress had used the Indian Queen as the country's earliest official symbol (see pages 62 and 64). Despite the criticism, the three-dollar gold coin remained in circulation for thirty-five years, widely known as the Indian Princess coin.

James Barton Longacre (1794–1869), designer. Indian-head three-dollar gold coin, 1854–89. Stamped gold, copper. Courtesy of the Numismatic Guaranty Corporation, Sarasota, Florida

IN JUNE 1860, the Ladies of Powhatan County, Virginia—the county that in 1777 the Virginia General Assembly had created and named in honor of Pocahontas's father— presented to Company E of the Fourth Virginia Cavalry this double-sided flag, which would be raised for service in the Confederate States Army (American Civil War Museum 2016). The Ladies of Powhatan County were likely the wives, mothers, sisters, and daughters of Powhatan County men enlisted in Company E of the volunteer regiment. One side of the flag (not illustrated) bears the emblem of the recently created Virginia state flag, a personification of Virtus, the Roman deity of bravery.

The other side, shown here, features a quasi-heraldic image. Although the makers of the original Virginia state flag did not want it to look like a British-style coat of arms, this side of the Powhatan Troop flag nonetheless resembles the banners of ancient European orders of knighthood that were made to advance royal or ecclesiastical causes. Its central image is a portrait of a young woman with flowing black hair meant to represent Pocahontas. Above and below her portrait are trompe l'oeil ribbons in which Company E's motto is inscribed (heraldic mottoes always appear on ribbons or scrolls).

Fighting as part of the Army of Northern Virginia, the Fourth Virginia Cavalry, including Company E, would participate in all the major Civil War campaigns, including the epic Battle of Gettysburg in 1863. The flag was clearly meant to identify Company E not simply with Virginia or even Powhatan County but also specifically with Pocahontas—that is, the young Powhatan woman whose father was the county's namesake and whose memory the Ladies of Powhatan County cherished. In their adulation of and identification with Pocahontas, the women created a flag that served as a noble exhortation for their soldiers.

Long before 1860, Pocahontas (ca. 1595–1617) had become a well-known historical figure for having supposedly saved the life in 1607 of Jamestown colonist Captain John Smith and, by extension, bringing success to the colony itself. In 1615, Ralph Hamor published *A True Discourse of the Present Estate of Virginia* . . . , in which he wrote about Pocahontas's abduction by the Jamestown settlers the year before. Hamor's book introduced her to a book-reading European audience. During the time the English had held her captive, Pocahontas had met the colonist John Rolfe, whom she married in 1614. Her marriage was heralded, and credited with bringing about a period of peace between the English and Powhatan. In 1616, when Pocahontas traveled to London with her husband, she was received at the court of King James I as an Indian princess. While abroad, her portrait was artistically rendered from life, engraved, and soon published in Compton Holland's *Bazilioologia: A Booke of Kings* (1618). In 1619, Theodore de Bry's son, Johann, republished Hamor's book. He also published volume 10 of *America* (see page 28), which included an account and engraving of Pocahontas's kidnapping as well as other illustrated incidents from her life.

Fourth Virginia Volunteer Cavalry Regiment, Company E, Powhatan Troop Flag, 1860–61. Oil on silk, metallic fringe. Courtesy of the American Civil War Museum, Richmond, Virginia

Less than two years after she had "entered the history books," Pocahontas died prematurely in 1617. Pocahontas's son, Thomas, only one year old when he lost his mother, was raised in London by his Rolfe relatives. When he returned to colonial Virginia in 1635, he became a prosperous tobacco planter and married into one of the colony's elite families. His descendants, who became influential in Virginia and nationally, kept Pocahontas's memory alive, much as other First Families of Virginia (those who descended from the original English colonists at Jamestown) maintained memories of their lineage founders. In 1839, twenty-two years before the outbreak of the American Civil War, a large painting titled *Baptism of Pocahontas* was installed in the rotunda of the U.S. Capitol as one of a series of works commemorating important events in U.S. history (see page 71). The painting sealed Pocahontas's position as one of the nation's founders.

The Ladies of Powhatan County may not have fully appreciated the irony of their county's being named after the powerful paramount chief of the coastal Algonquian confederacy that had dominated the Chesapeake Bay region when the English established James Fort in 1607—and that the English had destroyed by 1645. But no doubt they knew that during Pocahontas's lifetime, the English had feted her as an Indian princess, and indeed she had become a symbol of one. If the ladies' knowledge of the historical facts surrounding Pocahontas was weak and mired in their romantic adulation of Indian "royalty," it was nonetheless firmly anchored to the centrality of the young Powhatan woman to numerous consequential events in early seventeenth-century Virginia. Any unease about Pocahontas's indigenous origin was assuaged by her widely reported conversion to Christianity and the many subsequent allusions to it, as on the Powhatan Troop flag.

It is unknown whether any of the Ladies of Powhatan County traced their own family lines to Pocahontas. But in creating the Powhatan Troop flag in 1860, a year of increasing uncertainty about the fate of the republic, the women plainly were determined to assert their (symbolic or real) blood connection, via Pocahontas, to the country's very founding—and birthplace in the South. The flag stands out because of the motivation behind its creation, and the connection it draws between the events of 1860 and those of the early 1600s. This does not diminish the deeper political reasons for which the American Civil War was fought, nor the country's current concern over the public display of Confederate symbols. The flag highlights the vastly different ways in which Americans have invoked Pocahontas at crucial moments in U.S. history.

THE ORNATE, LUSTROUS, AND QUINTESSENTIALLY Victorian silver centerpiece known as the Hiawatha Boat was selected for the White House by First Lady Julia Dent Grant (Monkman 2000, 151–52; Allman and Naulin 2011, 34). She was the wife of Ulysses S. Grant, the Civil War hero and twenty-eighth president of the United States. The Grants occupied the White House from 1869 to 1877. Mrs. Grant saw the centerpiece when it was displayed at the 1876 Centennial Exposition in Philadelphia. The Gorham Manufacturing Company, the silversmithing firm that produced it, may have presented it to her there (Allman and Naulin 2011, 34).

The Hiawatha Boat consists of a rimmed tray supported by crouching bears and mirrored to evoke a lake. A single-mast canoe, in which sits an American Indian pilot, is flanked by sprays of wild grasses, bulrushes, and water lilies, further evoking the lake setting. The centerpiece depicts the story of Hiawatha that Henry Wadsworth Longfellow told in his epic poem of 1855, *The Song of Hiawatha*. Inscriptions from the poem are engraved on each side of the rimmed tray: "All Alone Went Hiawatha through the Clear, Transparent Water" and "Swift or Slow at Will He Glided, Veered to Right or Left at Pleasure." In the mid-nineteenth century, Longfellow was not only a major American poet and cultural figure but also a world-famous literary figure. The Hiawatha in Longfellow's widely read poem is a fictional character, not to be confused with the precolonial Haudenosaunee (Iroquois) leader associated with the founding of the Iroquois Confederacy.

The Hiawatha Boat was used as a table setting at state dinners during President Grant's and President Grover Cleveland's administrations (ibid. 2011, 34). Beginning with President Grant, state dinners took on their contemporary function as elaborate and prestigious affairs hosted by the president to welcome a visiting dignitary (Monkman 2016). Surrounded by a formal arrangement of shimmering presidential china and finely etched glassware bearing national symbols such as the eagle and the Great Seal of the United States, the Hiawatha Boat was given pride of place atop the magnificent fourteen-foot-long gilded-bronze table decoration known as the Monroe Plateau, which President James Monroe had brought to the United States from Paris. When not used for state dinners, the boat graced White House public parlors such as the Red Room and, later, the first family's dining room (Allman and Naulin 2011, 34; Monkman 2000, 152).

Longfellow's greatly loved *Song of Hiawatha* was loosely based upon Algonquian oral narratives concerning the figure Winneboujou (also called Manabus or Manabozo, depending on the dialect) as Henry Rowe Schoolcraft interpreted them in his *Myth of Hiawatha* (1856; see page 74). Schoolcraft, an early ethnographer, recorded numerous Ojibwe oral narratives, sometimes taking liberties in his effort to convey their poetic aesthetics.[1] In its day, Longfellow's *Song of Hiawatha* was lauded for its serious attempt to create radical versification (it forgoes rhyme) and a poetic and national literature. Set in the Midwest's northern lake country, the long narrative poem tells a "uniquely American" story, that of an American Indian in a natural setting who, at the poem's end, sings a "death song" not just for himself but also for the red race.

Longfellow was intent on penning a national epic fit for the United States that expressed its frontier history. During the mid-nineteenth century, a distinctly American literary tradition had yet to emerge. The acceptance of Longfellow's "American epic" as establishing such a tradition can be read not only in the poem's enduring appeal (it was required reading for American schoolchildren for decades, and generations of adults could recite long passages at length) but also in the prominent display of the Hiawatha Boat in the White House during the last twenty-five years of the 1800s.

Throughout American history, silver objects have been equated with prestige, status, and refinement. Like the finest colonial and federal-era silver, the White House's Hiawatha Boat was a magnificent object that epitomized stately homes of its era. Just as the Longfellow poem commemorating a "uniquely American" story embodied a deep contradiction, though, so did the Hiawatha Boat. Both the centerpiece and the poem ostensibly aspired to evoke a meaningful link between the experiences of Americans and American Indians, though neither made the connection successfully. A link was made, however, between Americans and nature on the one hand, and American Indians and the fringes of civilization on the other. Neither the poem nor the boat acknowledged, let alone bridged, the cultural and political chasm between the United States and American Indians that existed in the last quarter of the nineteenth century. The moral complexity that the Hiawatha Boat represented among the national symbols in the White House remained politely veiled in the well-mannered political and diplomatic circles that gathered there until, like Longfellow's epic, the brave-in-a-canoe centerpiece, a vessel for Victorian imaginations, was no longer considered fashionable.

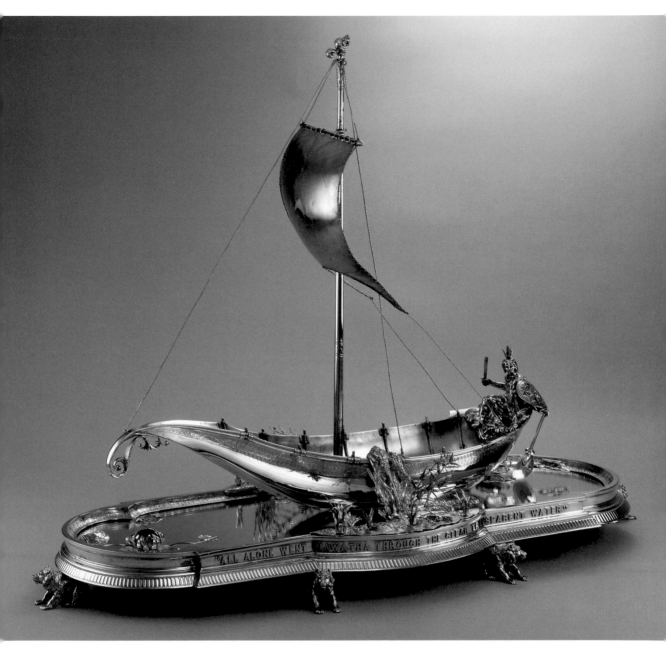

Gorham Manufacturing Company. Hiawatha Boat centerpiece, 1871. Silver. ©2000 White House Historical Association

THE IMPROVED ORDER OF RED MEN (IORM), which describes itself as "devoted to inspiring a greater love for the United States of America and the principles of American Liberty," is the oldest fraternal patriotic association in the United States. The organization traces its history to the prerevolutionary Sons of Liberty (see page 50). In 1812, it adopted the name Society of Red Men, then in 1834 became the Improved Order of Red Men. As its names imply, the group has always identified itself with American Indians—ostensibly with their governance structures, rituals, modes of dress, and values.

The most urgent challenge facing the Founding Fathers and first generations of Americans was to create a nation-sized republic fully committed to the ideal of self-representation. The IORM perceived the essential elements of representational democracy in American Indian societies, which members of the IORM emulated because they believed that Native nations fostered deliberation and consensus, the twin foundations on which self-government rests. How much the group understood about the functioning of individual American Indian societies, or of any aspects of American Indian cultures, has been effectively challenged (Deloria 1998, 38–70). Betraying their own weak grasp of American Indian institutions, the IORM wrote, "There was among them [American Indian societies] a similarity of ceremonies and customs which makes a description of the tribes inhabiting one part of country typical of all" (Lindsay [1893] 2015, 24). Nonetheless the IORM, a society devoted to liberty, intentionally organized itself around many supposed facets of American Indian life, including what it assumed to be American Indian values, to shape its own political identity. Considering themselves knowledgeable about American Indian tribes (the "primitive red men"), they singled out the Haudenosaunee, or Iroquois Confederacy, to emulate. As the IORM wrote in its official history, the league "achieved a remarkable civilized organization . . . [with] wisdom in their civil institutions and sagacity in [its] administration" (ibid., 32). To express its fascination for American Indians and their mode of self-governance, the IORM calls the holder of its highest post Great Chief and its officers hold titles such as Great Keeper of Wampum and Great Prophet. These titles refer to the Haudenosaunee custom of creating wampum belts to record and narrate history, traditions, and laws, and likely also to the Seneca prophet, Handsome Lake. IORM members are called warriors and braves. Local IORM meeting sites are called wigwams, and local chapters tribes (e.g., Lenne Lenape Tribe, Black Hawk Tribe, Ottawa Tribe, Sioux Tribe), which are presided over by sachems, a term referencing North American Indian chiefs. IORM members uphold the values of freedom, friendship, charity, and unity.

Improved Order of Red Men membership certificate, ca. 1889. Chromolithograph. Published by Burke and McFetridge. Courtesy of the Library of Congress Prints and Photographs Division LC-DIG-pga-03413

The Improved Order of Red Men's membership certificate of 1889 bears an uncanny resemblance to Theodore de Bry's engraving used on the title pages of volumes 3 and 4 of his *America* (see page 28). Whereas de Bry placed scenes of supposed American Indian cannibalism and idolatry in the niches of a classically inspired structure, the designer of the IORM certificate situated vignettes of American Indian life in a federal-era frame. The frame has eleven openings, or windows, and is especially ornate at the bottom, with a profusion of overlapping scrolls and foliage. Similar in design to formal mirror frames dating to the late eighteenth century, the IORM frame is surmounted by a bald eagle supporting a shield painted with thirteen red and white stripes representing the original states. The blue top of the shield represents Congress. It is inscribed with the letters T. O. T. E., for Totem of the Eagle, which the IORM artist added to the symbolic shield of the United States. The bald eagle is flanked by the U.S. and IORM flags, while busts of George Washington and Tammany flank the eagle-and-flag tableau. Clearly, George Washington and Tammany (see page 91) are equal in stature for the IORM. The picture planes for all ten American Indian vignettes are recessed, and each is vibrantly colored. The design of the certificate evokes the feel of a religious icon, which portrays scenes from the life of a revered saint. The American Indian images, however, are ill-executed and represent no identifiable Native society or event, other than the curiously presented landing of Christopher Columbus. Several scenes appear loosely based on George Catlin paintings dating to the 1830s and generically represent Plains Indian, but all are devoid of serious or sustained effort to convey cultural specificity. The scene depicting Christopher Columbus (bottom center) may have been conceived entirely by the artist. Each of the ten vignettes is accompanied by a banner on which is inscribed an entreaty to virtue attributed to American Indians, such as: "Be merciful to strangers found in the forest" and "It is the will of the Great Spirit that you reverence the aged."

In stringing together an array of the supposed American Indian dictums, the IORM in effect equated the values with its own love of liberty. But oddly, neither the IORM nor any of its predecessor patriotic societies saw a contradiction in promoting American Indian virtues but denying liberty to actual American Indians, as the nation endeavored to expand its territory. Their emulation of Americans Indians was fanciful. Still, so compelling were the IORM's commitment to the ideal of liberty and its regard for supposed American Indian values that three presidents of the United States were counted among its members: Theodore Roosevelt, inducted in 1906; Warren G. Harding, inducted in 1922; and Franklin D. Roosevelt, inducted when he was governor of New York, in 1930 (Davis 1990, 402, 360, 440).

Improved Order of Red Men membership certificate, ca. 1889 (details). Chromolithograph. Published by Burke and McFe- tridge. Courtesy of the Library of Congress Prints and Photographs Division LC–DIG–pga–03413

CIVIL WAR SCHOLAR James McPherson has described the Battle of Gettysburg as "the largest battle ever fought in the Western Hemisphere" (McPherson 2015, 1). The author points out that this three-day battle in 1863 resulted in ten times more American casualties than the D-Day invasion at Normandy in World War II (ibid., xiv). The Battle of Gettysburg was a decisive victory for the Union Army and turned the tide of the Civil War, but entire regiments disappeared under the barrage of cannon and musket artillery. Almost eleven thousand soldiers on both sides lost their lives, with more than twenty-nine thousand others wounded (McPherson 2015, ix). Four and a half months after the July battle, on November 9, 1863, President Abraham Lincoln paid tribute to the Union soldiers in his lauded Gettysburg Address. Besides memorializing the soldiers, Lincoln's speech at the Soldiers' National Cemetery in Gettysburg framed the Civil War as a fight for the preservation of the country envisioned by the Founding Fathers. A country, in Lincoln's words, with a "government of the people, by the people, and for the people."

A year after Lincoln delivered his address, the Gettysburg Battlefield Memorial Association was organized to protect the battlefield. In addition to preserving the field, they set aside land for Battle of Gettysburg monuments, which eventually numbered more than one thousand. Erected among them in 1891 was the monument to the Forty-Second New York Volunteer Infantry Regiment of the Union Army, also known as the Tammany Regiment, which the Tammany Society in New York City raised and organized in May and June 1861. The New York Tammany Society, a branch of a wider network of societies, was named for the Lenape (Delaware) chief Tammany, whom Revolutionary War colonists admired, even revered. The subject of the monumental bronze statue, Chief Tammany, stands in front of a tipi and atop a ten-foot-high granite pedestal. The monument's creator, American sculptor John J. Boyle, studied art under Thomas Eakins and in Paris at the École des Beaux-Arts. He received numerous prestigious commissions, including this monument.

Mention of the New York Tammany Society today conjures the corrupt Democratic political machine that back-room politicians operated in New York City during the nineteenth century. But the New York Tammany Society was founded in 1789 by American Revolutionary War veteran William Mooney. Known at different times as the Sons, or Society, of St. Tammany, or Tammany Hall, it was a fraternal and patriotic organization dedicated to antifederalist principals. Americans had joined together to a certain extent during the Revolutionary War to free themselves from the tyranny of the British, distant rulers who, they believed, could not possibly have their local interests in mind, as proven by the ruinous taxes they imposed (see page 46).

John J. Boyle (1852–1917). Monument to Forty-Second New York Volunteer Infantry "Tammany" Regiment, 1891. Bronze, granite. Randy Duchaine/Alamy Stock Photo

After the Revolutionary War, most Americans in the thirteen original states lived at great distances from one another, and many desired no higher form of government than that of their own town or county (Ellis 2015, vii). In the 1780s, many Americans, including members of the New York Tammany Society, opposed the Constitution and its ratification.[1] They alleged, in fact, that the Constitution (without significant amendments) was an aristocratic document (Ellis 2015, 3–28; Scigliano 2001, 24). Wanting to stay true to America's revolutionary ideals, they resisted any attempts to concentrate power at a national level, which they believed would open the door to an American monarchy.

Early antifederalists, including members of the Tammany Society, favored state sovereignty, a locally based governmental structure composed of citizens who understood and supported local interests and made decisions by consensus (Storing 1981, 7–14). They viewed distant sources of power as highly suspect (Ellis 2015, 12). Tammany Society members manifested their political models by emulating American Indian societies. They considered those societies to be untainted by absolute rule and based instead upon a natural form of self-representation. They even went so far as to adopt pseudo–American Indian dress at their meetings and refer to their officers by the term sachem. Their emulation was not, however, grounded in direct knowledge of American Indian political structures or peoples. Tellingly, the society took its name from the Lenape chief Tammend, or Tamanend, known for befriending the Quaker William Penn in the 1600s (see page 68).

Desiring a monument to the Tammany Regiment soldiers killed at Gettysburg, the society commissioned Boyle to create a statue of Chief Tammany. Boyle had come to the New York Tammany Society's attention after creating two earlier public commissions with American Indian subject matter. Both works portray Indians whose day has essentially come and gone. The first was a large-scale bronze sculpture titled *The Alarm*, made in 1884 for Lincoln Park in Chicago. Executed in a Beaux-Arts style, the work features an Ottawa Indian family (man, woman, and child). The Tammany Society was impressed with Boyle's close attention to physiognomy, texture, and (seemingly) realistic detail in this work. The second, *Stone Age in America*, was first exhibited in 1888 in Philadelphia and then at the World's Columbian Exposition in 1893. Boyle's realistic and naturalist depiction of a vigorous American Indian woman and her children represented the noble manner in which the society wanted their "St. Tammany" rendered.

Boyle's sculpture is an attempt at a large-scale bronze portrait. In creating his work, Boyle paid equal attention to facial expression, anatomical details, fringed hide clothing, and feather headdress. Tammany holds a bow, with his spears close at hand. The clothing and weapons are, of course, entirely wrong for a seventeenth-century Lenape Indian, as is the dwelling behind Tammany. The curiously flat-sided tipi, a type neither the Lenape nor any other Native society ever used, is as odd

John J. Boyle (1852–1917). Monument to Forty-Second New York Volunteer Infantry "Tammany" Regiment, 1891 (detail). Bronze, granite. Maurice Savage/Alamy Stock Photo

as the Tammany's Society's assumptions about American Indian rites, and its general inattentiveness to historical and cultural accuracy in regard to its namesake.

But—as has been done so often in visual expressions of national identity created at moments of jubilation, patriotism, or, in this case, profound national grief—the Tammany Society was putting forth a representation of an American Indian as a reminder of the ideals of the Founding Fathers: liberty and self-government. Likewise, the Tammany Society's monument draws a direct parallel between their regiment's sacrifice and the sacrifices of those who fought in the American Revolution, just as President Lincoln had done in the Gettysburg Address.

UNTIL 1869, EVERY U.S. POSTAGE STAMP honored a prominent and respected American such as Benjamin Franklin or George Washington (West 2014, 73). Beginning in that year, stamps were issued with figurative scenes that celebrated significant moments or singular achievements in U.S. history, such as the building of the transcontinental railroad. In 1898, the U.S. Postal Service issued a series of commemorative postage stamps to honor the American West, one of which was the first to feature an American Indian as the main subject rather than a passive bystander. It was titled *Indian Hunting Buffalo*. Published as part of the commemorative series made for the Trans-Mississippi and International Exposition held that year, the stamp presents a dramatic frontier image that the American public well knew from paintings by several of the country's most famous artists. Currier & Ives and other printers often reimagined works such as George Catlin's *Indian Hunt* from 1844 and John Mix Stanley's *Buffalo Hunt on the Southwestern Prairies* from 1845—and countless Americans bought the reproductions. The scene on the 1898 stamp is based on a painting, *Buffalo Chase*, that Seth Eastman made thirty years earlier (in the Collection of the U.S. House of Representatives) and the artist's engraving of the same scene, also titled *Buffalo Chase*. Eastman was a military officer and artist who was stationed at several frontier forts throughout his career (Boehme, Feest, and Johnston 1995, 2). While Eastman painted scenes of the West on his own accord, the federal government also often called upon him to illustrate its publications concerning Indians. The most famous of these is Henry Rowe Schoolcraft's *Historical and Statistical Information Respecting the History, Conditions, and Prospects of the Indian Tribes of the United States*, in which the engraving of *Buffalo Chase* first appeared (1854; see page 74).

In the mid-nineteenth century, while artists such as Catlin, Stanley, and Eastman were rendering their impressions of the West, the Great Plains were dominated by Indian peoples—Lakota, Cheyenne, Arapaho, Apsáalooke (Crow), Blackfeet, Mandan, Hidatsa, and Assiniboine, for example—whose religious beliefs and oral narratives exalted the power and majesty of the buffalo and acknowledged Native dependency on the buffalo for food, clothing, and shelter. The buffalo sustained Plains Indians spiritually as well as physically. By the time the *Indian Hunting Buffalo* stamp was issued in 1898, however, it had been almost ten years since the massacre at Wounded Knee, the Indian Wars had come to an end, and Plains Indians had been confined to reservations and rendered powerless in the minds of most Americans. Furthermore, Americans' industrial-scale hunting had long since depleted the once-vast herds of buffalo. So dependent was the American Industrial Revolution on buffalo hides to make conveyors and belts to propel machinery into mass-producing commercial products that the American bison was on the verge of extinction.

Yet the *Indian Hunting Buffalo* postage stamp of 1898 sparked American imaginations. It encapsulated the country's fixation on exploring and settling the West, the

***Indian Hunting Buffalo* four-cent stamp, 1898.** After Seth Eastman (1808–1875), *Buffalo Chase*, ca. 1850. Engraving. Courtesy of the National Postal Museum, Smithsonian Institution, Washington, DC

defining ambition of the United States since the days of Thomas Jefferson and the Lewis and Clark expedition (see page 151). While it is a fact that Plains Indians were hunters, it is a powerful myth that all American Indians were hunters only, knowing neither how to cultivate the ground nor productively exploit its natural resources (i.e., for profit). The buffalo-hunter image on the stamp lends itself perfectly to the myth. Tellingly, the stamp was issued to commemorate the Trans-Mississippi Exposition, a world's fair held in Omaha to celebrate the country's development in the West. Other stamps in the set of nine featured subjects such as cattle, prospectors, and pioneers (West 2014, 98). Paradoxically yet effortlessly, the *Indian Hunting Buffalo* stamp, a dramatic frontier image turned into an indelible national emblem, epitomizes nineteenth-century America and its unbridled national ambitions to explore, map, settle, cultivate, and ultimately exploit the land. Recounted with such gusto were stories of winning the West that, in 1898, the social and political assault on Plains Indians, their struggles to maintain their land, the diminishment of their populations, and their subjugation merited no more attention from the American public, as far as the U.S. Postal Service was concerned, than the nostalgic nod to the past expressed in its four-cent *Indian Buffalo Hunt* stamp.

Daniel Chester French (1850–1931). *The Continents: America,* **1903–07.** Tennessee marble. NMAI
Photo Services, Smithsonian Institution, Washington, DC

THE ALEXANDER HAMILTON U.S. CUSTOM HOUSE was built by the federal government in New York City between 1902 and 1907 to house the duty-collection operations of the Port of New York. Designed by architect Cass Gilbert, the building is considered a masterpiece of the Beaux-Arts style. Prominently placed across the front of the building, as Gilbert envisioned, are four magnificent sculptures by Daniel Chester French, who had undertaken numerous prominent federal commissions and would later count among his most famous works the statue of Abraham Lincoln, completed in 1920, for the Lincoln Memorial in Washington, DC. French's U.S. Custom House sculptures represent female allegorical figures of the continents of Asia, America, Europe, and Africa.

The figure of America is a strong, vigilant, and forward-looking young woman who seemingly portrays an ideal: she holds the torch of progress in her right hand. Her right foot, placed upon the head of Quetzalcoatl, a Mixteca (Aztec) deity, righteously stamps out the Americas' indigenous religions while the eagle, a symbol of American power and authority, is discreetly perched to her right. On the left side of America is a kneeling, bare-chested man holding tools.

On America's lap rests a large bushel of corn, a "New World" crop representing a nation that identified itself with agricultural strength. Ironically, indigenous peoples throughout the Americas had, before the arrival of Europeans, not only farmed extensively but also developed hybrids of corn that they cultivated at different altitudes and under various climatic conditions. In North, Central, and South America, Native farmers had devised ingenious hydraulic systems ranging from directing rainfall to carefully chosen field locations (Dominguez and Kolm 2005, 732) to carving horizontal terraces for farming along steep mountainsides (Barreiro 2015, 3). They devised expansive and integrated raised-platform field farming to protect crops from flooding, while surrounding them with canals to provide irrigation when necessary (Morehart 2016, 184). They modified soil texture and chemical properties to increase agricultural productivity (Woodson 2015, 271). Long before Europeans and others arrived in the Western Hemisphere, these and other sophisticated agricultural practices allowed American Indians to grow corn in arid or flood zones (as well as along rich alluvial plains), support large populations and ritual events, and produce surpluses for markets and future needs. Corn, beans, and squash (together with potatoes and other agricultural crops) were critically important to the diets of American Indians. Scientists today, including those working at the U.S. Department of Agriculture, now recognize the widespread and ancient practice of mixed cropping (or intercropping, by which different crops are planted sequentially in the same field) provided American Indians with a stable and sustainable agricultural system (Mt. Pleasant 2006, 529; Whitcomb 2015).

At the turn of the twentieth century, however, Americans knew nothing of the long history of American Indian agricultural innovation. French's grand allegory of America deliberately includes a Plains Indian man. Immediately identifiable by his eagle-feather headdress, he is just visible over America's right shoulder. Hugely symbolic, he represents the quintessential American Indian hunter. Throughout U.S. history, what Americans saw as American Indians' inability to use the land productively arose from their insistence that American Indians were "children of the forest," "nomadic," "unsettled," "wanderers," or "marauders." Considering them ignorant of farming made it easier for Americans to regard American Indians as an obstacle to America's westward expansion and burgeoning capitalism. Unabashedly, French's allegorical sculpture and its placement on a building devoted to one of the most fundamental of U.S. government activities—regulating compliance with trade laws—speaks volumes about American attitudes toward American Indians and the land (see page 65).

Europeans have long used allegorical figures to personify the continents (see page 30). Ironically, when they first encountered America, as they soon called the Western Hemisphere, they personified it as an American Indian Princess or Queen (Fleming 1965, 65). This custom persisted through the sixteenth, seventeenth, and eighteenth centuries. In the early eighteenth century, the British used the image of a young, healthy, vigorous American Indian woman to represent the thirteen British colonies (see page 46). The graphic representation changed, however, once the colonies became rebellious. The Indian Princess became unruly and unkempt. When the United States was established, the Founding Fathers reimagined the allegory yet again. She became an American Indian Queen, classical in her anatomical proportions, face, pose, and garb (see page 62). It was an image befitting a new republic.

The sculptor's allegory of America in *The Continents: America* was intended to represent the Western Hemisphere's past, present, and future, but it signifies only one country, the United States. Here, the symbol of America, or the United States, is no longer a female American Indian. The Indian Queen has been replaced by a Caucasian woman. The United States was built on the notion that it was the land of opportunity for white (or Euro-American) settlers and pioneers; the inclusion of the American Indian in French's magisterial sculpture embodies the United States' understanding and justification of its past. But the real focus here is America at the dawn of a new century. Assured in her purpose and destiny, she looks straight out to the future. The secondary story captures the country's widespread but mistaken belief in the notion of the vanquished American Indian, resigned to his fate and showing no signs of political resistance, who cannot but peer over America's shoulder.

Keystone View Company and B. L. Singley. *Indian Chiefs headed by Geronimo, passing in review before President Roosevelt, Inauguration Day, 1905, Washington, D.C., U.S.A.* Stereograph. Courtesy of Library of Congress Prints and Photographs Division, LC-DIG-stereo-1s02197

ATTUNED TO THE SPIRIT OF TRIUMPHALISM pervading the United States at the turn of the twentieth century (the United States had just won the Spanish-American and Philippine-American Wars), Theodore Roosevelt arranged to have six American Indian leaders, a "delegation of conquered Indian chiefs" (*New York Times* 1905, 1), headline the inaugural parade following his swearing-in ceremony and luncheon on March 4, 1905. In revealing his desire to include Quanah Parker (Comanche), Charles Buck (Ute), Hollow Horn Bear (Sicangu [Brulé] Lakota), Little Plume (Blackfeet), and Geronimo (Chiricahua Apache) in his parade, Roosevelt explained that for his second inauguration he "wanted to give the people a good show."

At best, by positioning American Indian leaders whose names had once blazed across newspapers in every state of the nation as a spectacle before the American people, Roosevelt was ushering in a new era for the country by paying tribute to its past. He was defining the turn of the century as a hinge moment by celebrating the uniquely American national identity that had been forged out of the nineteenth-century frontier experience, itself largely defined by the Indian Wars. But seen from today's perspective, Roosevelt's inclusion of "conquered Indian chiefs" in his inaugural parade was a curious if not questionable act of political theater.

Stereographs were the most popular photographic format of the late nineteenth and early twentieth centuries. Produced by the millions, they were viewed at home in the comfort of one's parlor through hand-held devices that allowed the viewer to perceive a single three-dimensional image when looking at two side-by-side photographic prints of the same subject taken from slightly different angles of perspective. In the days before reprinting photographs in newspapers and magazines was possible, the market for stereographs was tremendous. The Keystone View Company, the world's largest distributor of stereographs in 1905, clearly felt it had a marketable image that captured an extraordinary historical event. According to the *New York Times*, Roosevelt's inauguration drew the "greatest outside crowd to the nation's seat of government that has ever been brought there" (ibid.). Countless others, unable to share directly in the excitement of the Washington, DC, throngs, could then view the Indian leaders headlining Roosevelt's parade through the next best means then available—through a form of communication "that exceeded everything known before it" (Newhall [1982] 2009, 85).

The Keystone View Company stereograph did record a truly historical and uniquely American occasion. It did not capture, however, the fact that as the six Native leaders paraded past an ebullient Roosevelt—standing "alone in the wind, waving his tall hat, bowing, clapping and laughing" (Morris 2001, 377)—they and their people were dealing with myriad detrimental circumstances. Waves of epidemics were ravaging reservations across the country, causing populations to decline perilously. A transition to wage labor and a cash economy was resulting, albeit unintentionally, in economic marginalization. Assaults upon Native leadership structures were causing divisive tribal disputes. Throughout, Native children were being taken away to boarding schools without their parents' consent. What the Keystone View Company stereograph of Roosevelt's inaugural parade did not show was American Indians' ongoing struggles for social justice.

These struggles were led by forward-thinking Native men and women who rejected a federal policy bent on destroying the foundation of their social, spiritual, economic, and political lives. Their immediate concerns were the survival of their communities, protection of their remaining lands, and increasing their political powers vis-à-vis autocratic Indian agents (Hoxie 2012, 4). If their communities were not already on the verge of collapse, the Native activists were working at the community level, as well as intertribally and even nationally to avoid the possibility that it might happen. They took issue with a number of harsh government efforts that were detrimental to their societies (Hoxie 2001b, 1–28). Geronimo, Hollow Horn Bear, and Quanah Parker, especially, had clear understandings of the challenges and hardships facing their communities. On March 9, five days after the parade, they

Keystone View Company and B. L. Singley. *Indian Chiefs headed by Geronimo, passing in review before President Roosevelt, Inauguration Day, 1905, Washington, D.C., U.S.A.* (detail). Stereograph. Courtesy of Library of Congress Prints and Photographs Division, LC–DIG–stereo–1s02197

met with President Roosevelt. Through an interpreter, Geronimo pleaded for his people to be released from captivity. The U.S. Army had held them as prisoners of war at various military installations for nineteen years. After some discussion, the president told Geronimo, "It's best that you stay where you are" (Debo 1976, 421). Chiricahua Apaches would be detained for eight more years (see page 128).

As the Keystone View Company stereograph demonstrates, American Indians were deeply embedded in visual expressions of U.S. national identity in the early twentieth century. But on March 4, 1905, that identity was of a nation-state completely caught up in its power to shape its own destiny.

IN 1904, PRESIDENT THEODORE ROOSEVELT called upon the distinguished sculptor Augustus Saint-Gaudens to design a coin with an image of Liberty wearing a Plains Indian eagle-feather headdress. Roosevelt's rationale was that "on at least one coin we ought to have the Indian feather headdress. *It is distinctly American and very picturesque*" (Burdette 2007, 84–85; emphasis added). Upon Saint-Gaudens's death in 1907, the commission for the U.S. Indian-head half-eagle gold coin passed to American sculptor Bela Lyon Pratt. Pratt's design clearly depicts the head of a Native man, as opposed to a female personification of Liberty, and he is wearing a mostly accurate representation of a Plains Indian eagle-feather headdress. The artist's proposal succeeded in creating the visual effect Roosevelt wanted, and the half-eagle Indian-head coin was minted from 1908 to 1929.

By the time the Indian-head coin was designed and put into circulation, the eagle-feather headdress had become the iconic image of the Plains Indian warrior. More than any other article of clothing or ritual adornment, the headdress became the quintessential signifier of Plains Indians, likely for two principal reasons. First, throughout North America, American Indians traditionally were guided by leaders who could inspire and coordinate collective efforts through their oratory and judgment. The leaders' political and ceremonial authority was based upon their knowledge of their society's spiritual, philosophical, and ethical thought, the use of which sustained relationships between human society and the spiritual and natural worlds, as well as among groups like and unlike their own. In effect, their authority rested on their understandings of kinship. Further, American Indian societies generally developed strong connections between the clothing people wore and the spirit and animal worlds. Native leaders' headdresses often embodied profound spiritual and metaphysical meanings. They were regarded as powerful outward expressions of deeply held beliefs concerning interconnections among the human, animal, natural, and spiritual worlds. Additionally, the headdresses were symbols of ability and achievement and, at their most fundamental level, represented a people's right to govern and instruct themselves according to their own customs, beliefs, and laws.

The second probable explanation of how the headdress came to be the essential symbol of Plains Indians during the nineteenth century is that certain leaders of the Plains Indians (e.g., Lakota, Cheyenne, Arapaho, Apsáalooke [Crow], and Blackfeet) wore magnificent eagle-feather headdresses, often with impressively lengthy red wool and eagle-feather trains. Eagle-feather headdresses were worn by men of high standing whose stature was acknowledged and respected within their extended kin groups, camp circles, and nations.[1] Broadly speaking, eagles as solitary raptors were regarded as possessing desirable attributes, such as swiftness, assuredness, and dominance, that a leader wanted to possess in battle. The spiritual and ritual use of eagle feathers in Plains Indian life is perhaps most powerfully mani-

Bela Lyon Pratt (1867–1917), designer. Indian-head half-eagle gold coin, 1909. Engraved gold and copper. Courtesy of the Numismatic Guaranty Corporation, Sarasota, Florida

fested in the creation and donning of eagle-feather headdresses. The right of a man to wear such a headdress rested upon his ability to distinguish himself in battle and through his high moral standing.[2] Bravery in warfare was recognized as requiring intelligence, leadership, and honor (Medicine Crow 2003, 8). Further, men who wore eagle-feather headdresses were also acknowledged for exhibiting certain fundamental values. For Lakotas, these values include integrity, respect, wisdom, humility, generosity, and compassion (McDonnell 2009) and were regarded as being absolute requirements for becoming a chief or otherwise garnering respect. In other words, a man earned the right to wear an eagle-feather headdress through every aspect of his behavior.

But as President Roosevelt's reading of the Plains Indian eagle-feather headdress demonstrates, the American public had little appreciation for the social and spiritual significance of the headdress. The increasingly widespread use of the image in American popular culture speaks to its sheer visual power. In the hands of Americans, it became a reductive, though potent, symbol of Plains Indian warriors. Its use in popular culture has never conveyed the many other qualities that a man was required to demonstrate to achieve respect within his society and to become an esteemed leader.

In 1907, when President Roosevelt appears to have decided it was finally a propitious time to combine an American Indian headdress with Liberty on a U.S. coin, he was evidently unaware that this had already been done on a three-dollar coin in 1854 (see page 78). The symbolic association of representations of American Indians with Liberty had also been profoundly important for the American revolutionary generation and nation's Founding Fathers.

IN 1911, THE U.S. CONGRESS appropriated $275,000 for construction of the 261-foot-long, Romanesque Revival, five-arch Dumbarton Bridge in Washington, DC, designed by the distinguished architect Glenn Brown. Begun in 1914 and completed the next year, the bridge features fifty-six sculpted heads of Kicking Bear (Oglala/Minneconjou Lakota), a spiritual leader and veteran of the Battle of the Little Bighorn. Brown poetically described the bridge, which crosses the Rock Creek and Potomac Parkway, as spanning the "deep ravine of Rock Creek" (Brown and Brown 1915, 273), which at the time separated Georgetown from the heart of Washington.

Brown was a prominent Washington architect, highly regarded architectural historian, and a founding officer of the American Institute of Architects. One of his greatest legacies is widely considered to be his two-volume *History of the United States Capitol*, published in 1900 and 1903 (Bushong 2008, 1).[1] Brown was keen to design the Dumbarton Bridge for several reasons. First, Washington, DC, had recently embarked on a City Beautiful program and wanted the Dumbarton Bridge to be an architectural statement befitting the nation's capital. The commission for the design would be based upon the recommendation of a committee of architects, engineers, and sculptors constituting the city's new Commission of Fine Arts—making it a prestigious and visible project.[2] Second, the bridge would be located in a natural setting, and Brown wanted the challenge of designing a bridge in harmony with the natural site. It was to span rock outcroppings on two sides of a forested landscape in Washington's 1,800-acre Rock Creek Park. It would be an engineering challenge.

After determining that the bridge needed to be curved and that he wanted it to be made from a reddish brown sandstone reinforced with concrete, Brown based his design most directly on ancient Roman aqueducts and a certain bridge in a mountainous region of Italy that, he felt, elegantly used corbels (cantilevers that support weight) to brace its arches (Brown and Brown 1915, 275). On the Dumbarton Bridge, the Kicking Bear heads constitute the corbels supporting its balustrade. The idea grew out of Brown's study of ancient Maya architecture in the Yucatan and Central America (Brown and Brown 1915, 277), in which sculpted heads of deities and noblemen are often used as architectural elements on their temples and palace buildings.

The noted sculptor Alexander Phimister Proctor, best known for his ability to sculpt animals, was commissioned to create the Kicking Bear heads as well as two large buffalo at either end of the bridge. The Indian-head sculptures were meant to contribute to the "beauty of line, proportion of masses, fitness and scale in the details" of the bridge (Brown and Brown 1915, 273) and its American character. Incidentally, they are not the only American Indian design elements on the bridge.

Alexander Phimister Proctor (1860–1950). Sculpture from life mask of Kicking Bear, 1915. Kingwood stone. Courtesy of the Library of Congress Prints and Photographs Division, HAER DC, WASH, 594-8

In addition to the buffalo, each of the two niches on the pedestals for the buffalo has a small bas-relief of a quiverful of arrows draped with a feather headdress.

The Kicking Bear heads were created from a life mask of Kicking Bear made by the U.S. National Museum (now the Smithsonian's National Museum of Natural History). Life masks are the impression or mold of the face of a living person, usually made by oiling the skin and taking a plaster cast of the features (Bassett and Fogelman 1997, 27, 52). A life mask is generally produced for artistic use, as a model for a portrait based on a person's actual features. But the Kicking Bear life cast was made purely for anthropological purposes. At the turn of the twentieth century, Western anthropologists frequently made life casts of indigenous people worldwide. They were motivated by a nineteenth-century idea that race equated to social and mental development, a belief that went hand in hand with the concept of the "primitive man." According to Dr. Walter Hough, a curator at the U.S. National Museum, Kicking Bear's life cast was made when the Lakota leader visited Washington, DC, in 1896 (Hough 1920, 626). Hough discusses the event in his article, "Racial Groups and Figures in the Natural History Building of the United States National Museum," published in 1920 in the *Annual Report of the Board of Regents of the Smithsonian Institution*. The life cast was used to create a Lakota Warrior mannequin that was displayed in Hough's exhibition of "racial groups" (see Hough 1920).

Hough and his anthropological mentor, Alden Mason, were adherents of nineteenth-century social evolutionary theory and believed that American Indians, like other indigenous peoples, were inferior to Caucasians. Hough felt that the human mind provided a pathway into the primitive world. He saw people's social groupings, or cultures, as tied not only to their mentalities but also to every aspect of their material world. When studied and displayed "scientifically," those cultural groupings/mindsets/material worlds could reveal a "'series of ever perfecting thoughts' for which the human mind was no more than a constantly evolving agent of expression that led man inexorably to a condition approaching 'most nearly to the mind and life of the Creator'" (Hinsley Jr. 1981, 89). Hough's racial groupings laid out evolutionary stages for the "unfolding of culture as neither haphazard nor chaotic, but a gradual working out by human hands and minds" (ibid.). He and his colleagues at the Smithsonian's National Museum had no interest in the reasons Kicking Bear and his fellow Lakota were visiting Washington. They were focused on documenting a "vanishing race" and the social evolutionary stage of mankind to which it belonged.

Kicking Bear, however, did not visit as a representative of a vanishing race. A respected veteran of several well-known battles, he was also a leader of the Ghost Dance religion.[2] He was in Washington with a Lakota delegation that included Little Wound, George Fire Thunder, Captain Thunder Bear, and an interpreter. According to the *Evening Star* newspaper, "A task of greater magnitude to which the delegation of Sioux Indians now in the city is applying itself could not easily be imagined" (*Evening Star* 1896, 2). The delegation had several issues to address with government officials, among them that the United States was not honoring the treaty it had made with the Lakota. The delegates wanted the United States to restore reservation lands it had taken without Lakota knowledge.

Since 1973, the Dumbarton Bridge has been listed on the U.S. National Register of Historic Places (NRHP), meaning its "age, integrity, and significance" merits its identification as a national and "historic place worthy of preservation." One of the criteria for determining a structure's significance is whether the people connected with it were important in the past. The NRHP application acknowledged that the corbels of the bridge are stylized heads "modeled on a life mask of Kicking Bear, an American chief," but it is unknown whether Glenn Brown was aware that Kicking Bear had participated in the Battle of Little Bighorn and the Ghost Dance movement, or if he knew the import of Kicking Bear's visit to Washington. It is known that Brown wanted the sculptures of Kicking Bear's head to make an architectural statement; perhaps that was his only interest. Nevertheless, it matters greatly today to know who Kicking Bear was, why he was in Washington, and why the U.S. National Museum made a life cast of him. Only then can one begin to appreciate not only the grandeur but also the poignancy of the Dumbarton Bridge.

Glenn Brown (1854–1932). Dumbarton Bridge, 1915. Kingwood stone and concrete. Courtesy of the Library of Congress Prints and Photographs Division, HAER DC, WASH, 594-6

IN THE YEAR BEFORE the United States entered World War I, when aerial combat was in its infancy, 265 young American men volunteered to be trained as pilots and fight for France in the French air service, or Aéronautique Militaire. Although assigned to different squadrons, the pilots were most famously associated with the Lafayette Escadrille, or Lafayette Squadron, in which American pilots far outnumbered their French counterparts. It was first named the Escadrille Americaine but later renamed in honor of the Marquis de Lafayette, the French aristocrat and officer who fought for the United States during the American Revolutionary War. Each pilot of the Lafayette Escadrille, which first saw action during the Battle of Verdun in May 1916, hand painted an individual design on his biplane's canvas fuselage—until the fall of 1916, when an Indian-head insignia was added to all squadron biplanes. It was chosen for the "threatening expression" of the "savage Sioux" in the image (Thenault 1921, 103).

The insignia illustrated here belonged to Harold Buckley Willis, who became the twenty-fifth of thirty-eight Americans who flew with the Lafayette Escadrille. The green diagonal strip is unique to Willis's insignia. When the Lafayette Escadrille passed out of existence on February 18, 1918, many of its American pilots transferred to the newly organized 103rd Aero Squadron of the American Air Service, as did the Indian-head insignia.

The dramatic Lafayette Escadrille Indian-head insignia is reminiscent of the rousing, mass-produced, four-color lithographic posters created to advertise the immensely popular Wild West shows that swept across the United States and Europe between about 1883 and 1913. Those eagerly attended displays often ended with a reenactment of the Battle of Little Bighorn of 1876. Posters of Wild West performances, designed to capture the public's imagination, often re-created intense scenes that were ostensibly from that battle. They portrayed Plains Indians wearing eagle-feather headdresses, intent on warfare, fearlessly charging into a pitched battle. During World War I, the Savage Arms Company sold ammunition in boxes painted with an Indian-head logo, the face of which was stylistically indistinguishable from those of the Plains Indian warriors depicted on Wild West posters. The Lafayette Escadrille Indian-head logo is virtually identical to the Savage Arms logo. The dramatic Wild West shows and their posters created an image of daring Plains Indian warriors so resonant and widely seen that they were almost certainly the inspiration for the Savage Arms logo and, later, the Lafayette Escadrille squadron insignia.

The irony of the air corps' enthusiastic adoption of the Indian-head motif was that in the cold, wet, squalid, bloody, and perpetually crumbling trenches, roughly twelve thousand American Indian soldiers were trying to protect themselves from fragmenting projectiles with three-and-a-half-pound steel helmets. Most American Indians would not be recognized as U.S. citizens until 1924; nonetheless, American

Indian-head insignia used on French Lafayette Escadrille biplanes, 1917. Linen fabric, varnish, paint. Courtesy of the National Air and Space Museum, Smithsonian Institution, Washington, DC A19630014000

American aviator Robert Soubiran stands beside a Nieuport Type 17 pursuit plane featuring the Indian-head insignia, ca. 1917. A mechanic stands by the propeller. Courtesy of the National Air and Space Museum, Smithsonian Institution, Washington, DC (NASM 00175805)

Indians were drafted into and enlisted in the U.S. Army in astonishing numbers to fight in World War I (U.S. Department of Veterans Affairs 2012, 4). Artillery had become more effective and lethal than it had been in the past, so beginning with that war all U.S. ground troops wore protective steel helmets (National Research Council 2014, 11). While members of the Lafayette Escadrille and 103rd Aero Squadron derived their ideas about fearlessness in warfare from nineteenth-century imagery of Plains Indian warriors—which generated an insignia that helped eternalize an image that would come to signify all American Indians—unbeknownst to them American Indian soldiers from tribes throughout the United States were fighting in the trenches along the Western Front.

Among those soldiers were several fully bilingual Choctaw code talkers of the U.S. Army's Thirty-Sixth Division, 142nd Regiment. In late 1918, using technology new to the battlefield, they relayed coded radio and telephone transmissions that made possible the safe withdrawal of two companies from dangerous positions at Chufilly and Chardeny, France. That task is considered to have been the first crucial assignment for American Indian code talkers. Other code talkers' messages subsequently enabled a pivotal surprise attack that helped bring about the end of World War I; Armistice was signed a little more than two weeks after those transmissions. Before the U.S. Army began using American Indian code talkers, the German army had been able to break every American code developed for radio and telephone communications. After the war, France awarded its highest military honor, the Croix de Guerre, to ten American Indian soldiers, and an estimated one hundred others received medals for valor in battle in the war that defined modern warfare. But still, the mental image most Americans had of American Indians was tied to a nineteenth-century battle and the Wild West shows that capitalized on it.

Marine Corps officer's winter field coat with Indian–head–and–star patch 1919. Courtesy of the National Museum of the Marine Corps, Triangle, Virginia

THE INSIGNIA most widely associated with the U.S. Marine Corps, and the one most steeped in its history, is that of the eagle, globe, and anchor. But during World War I, a lesser known insignia was adopted when four regiments of U.S. Marines were deployed to France to join allied forces fighting the German military, serving as part of the Second Division of the American Expeditionary Forces (AEF). As part of the AEF, the marines were ordered to wear army field uniforms. Toward the end of the war, their uniform included a distinctive division insignia: a cloth shoulder patch with the profile of an American Indian wearing an eagle-feather headdress against a five-pointed star. Members of the Fourth Infantry Brigade (made up of the Fifth and Sixth Marine Regiments) who were attached to the Second Division did not keenly embrace the army uniform (Cody 2008, 36), but they willingly wore the Indian-head-and-star insignia. It is seldom associated with the marines today.

The Second Division had adopted the Indian-head-and-star insignia to distinguish its equipment from that of its allies (Joyce 1988, 66–72). Near the town of

Souilly in northeastern France, the Second Division's commanding officer held a competition among the enlisted men to create a distinctive insignia for that purpose. One soldier came up with a bold white star and another with the profile of an Indian wearing an eagle-feather headdress. The commanding officer combined the two. He approved a red, white, and blue Indian head against a white star, which on April 14, 1918, was immediately emblazoned on Second Division vehicles (ibid., 66). Its use eventually spread to uniforms worn by officers as well as enlisted men. By that time, differently shaped backgrounds (squares, diamonds, and ovals) of various colors (red, blue, yellow, green, and white) distinguished the units. Ultimately, sixty-eight variations on the insignia were in use (ibid., 71). The commanding general of the Second Division formally approved the Indian-head-and-star shoulder insignia on November 6, 1918.

The Indian head was modeled after the Indian-head five-dollar coin then in circulation (see page 102). The commanding officer for the Second Division deemed the insignia appropriate when it was first conceived because, as he said, there is "no need to remind anyone of the significance of the Indian . . . the first, and only true, and original American" (quoted in Joyce 1988, 66). After the war and upon returning to the states, soldiers and marines were instructed not to wear the insignia, as unit insignia were no longer considered important. Their attachment to the Indian-head-and-star insignia, however, led some marines in the Fifth and Sixth Marine Regiments to affix their shoulder insignia to the front of their helmets when they participated in Armistice Day parades (Cody 2008, 37). Their fondness for it resulted in an official request to permanently authorize the insignia. In 1920, the War Department adopted it for the Regular Army, the National Guard, and the National Army (Joyce 1988, 71).

The readily embraced and widespread use of the Indian-head-and-star insignia by marines of the Second Division and the War Department can be read two ways: as the adoption and proliferation of the Plains warrior stereotype, or as belief in the statement that American Indians are the "first, and only true, and original American." Those words should be considered in the context of World War I, when about twelve thousand American Indian men and women were drafted or enlisted in the U.S. military and participated in the AEF in France. The words reflect Americans' awareness of the primacy of American Indians in what became the United States. They also mirror a poignant reality: by the early twentieth century, the U.S. military was no longer fighting American Indians—as late nineteenth-century newspapers had vividly portrayed—but instead was fighting side-by-side, and identifying, with them.

Marine Corps uniform items worn during World War I victory parades. Indian-head-and-star shoulder patch, 1918–19; helmet with Indian-head-and-star insignia, 1918–19; officer's winter field coat with Indian-head-and-star patch, 1919 (detail). Courtesy of the National Museum of the Marine Corps, Triangle, Virginia

AMERICAN MILITARY AND POLITICAL LEADERS as well as the American public knew of the Sicangu (Brulé) Lakota chief Mat ó Hé lo e a, or Hollow Horn Bear, as early as 1866. Upon his death in 1913, he was accorded a funeral in the nation's capital that was attended by President Woodrow Wilson. Ten years later, the U.S. Postal Service issued a fourteen-cent stamp bearing the Lakota chief's visage. During his lifetime, Hollow Horn Bear had been photographed by several of the country's leading photographers, including Edward S. Curtis. His likeness on the postage stamp is based on a picture taken in 1905 by Bureau of American Ethnology photographer De Lancey W. Gill. That year Hollow Horn Bear had traveled to Washington, DC, to participate in President Theodore Roosevelt's inaugural parade (see page 99). Before the *Hollow Horn Bear* stamp appeared, the only other identifiable American Indian honored on a U.S. postage stamp had been Pocahontas.

As a follower of Chief Red Cloud (Oglala Lakota), Hollow Horn Bear was involved in pressuring the U.S. Army into abandoning three forts it had built along the Bozeman Trail, the wagon road built across Lakota and Cheyenne territory in present-day Wyoming and Montana that had allowed settlers to access the gold fields of Montana. In 1866, as Chief Red Cloud was negotiating with U.S. government peace commissioners to ameliorate the situation caused by the intrusion of settlers and soldiers, the army started constructing three additional forts along the trail, which dismayed and outraged Red Cloud. In November 1866, Captain William Judd Fetterman and eighty soldiers under his command invaded Lakota territory. Fetterman and his entire unit died in the ensuing battle, in which Hollow Horn Bear participated. Hollow Horn Bear later fought alongside Crazy Horse (Oglala Lakota) and Gall (Hunkpapa Lakota) in the still more infamous Battle of Little Bighorn of 1876, during which the U.S. Civil War hero Lieutenant Colonel George A. Custer and the entire Seventh Cavalry lost their lives.

After Little Bighorn, Hollow Horn Bear devoted himself to easing living conditions for the Lakota on the Rosebud Reservation, seeking to relax federal government restrictions. Still a legendary figure in the minds of Americans, he was asked to participate in not only President Theodore Roosevelt's inaugural parade in 1905 but also President Woodrow Wilson's in 1913. Hollow Horn Bear died of pneumonia while still in Washington after the latter.

Hollow Horn Bear's portrait on a national stamp constituted, after a fashion, the United States' acknowledgment of him as a Lakota warrior and worthy opponent. Identified on the stamp not as Hollow Horn Bear but as American Indian, he was honored for being an American Indian leader who "not only evaded death many times," as the *New York Times* (1913, 8) wrote in his obituary, but also fought fearlessly in battle and civilian life to protect his nation's territory and way of life. The obituary described Hollow Horn Bear as a man who was "born a pagan [and] . . . died a Christian," as that no doubt comforted many Americans for a host of reasons.

***Hollow Horn Bear* fourteen-cent stamp, 1923.** Engraving. Courtesy of the National Postal Museum, Smithsonian Institution, Washington, DC

By participating in two of the U.S. Army's most spectacular defeats—the Fetterman Fight and the Battle of Little Bighorn—Hollow Horn Bear became one of the American Indian figures who symbolized a frontier history that was becoming memorialized as unique to the United States and, even more fundamentally, as forging the American character. Capturing Hollow Horn Bear's dignity on a U.S. postage stamp in 1923, the country was, in effect, elevating a valiant foe to yet further aggrandize its westward expansion.

President Calvin Coolidge wears an eagle-feather headdress, 1927. State Game Lodge, South Dakota.
Photo by Leslie Jones. Courtesy of the Leslie Jones Collection, Boston Public Library

CALVIN COOLIDGE, THE THIRTIETH PRESIDENT of the United States, was mocked in the press (in his day and subsequently) for formally posing in the eagle-feather headdress that the daughter of Chauncey Yellow Robe (Sicangu [Brulé] Lakota) presented to him at a Lakota adoption ceremony on August 5, 1927 (*New York Times* 1927a, 19; 1927b, 159; 1927c, 1, 3). Yellow Robe, a great-nephew of Sitting Bull, had long been an advocate for the recognition of American Indians as U.S. citizens and continued to speak out for their acceptance as full and equal members of American society, even after they became citizens in 1924. That Coolidge was adopted into the Lakota Nation and made an honorary chief was seriously, though fleetingly, questioned on constitutional grounds. However ridiculous Silent Cal (as the president was nicknamed) may have appeared to some reporters, and whatever flap may have been caused by his adoption by the descendants of Indians who defeated Lieutenant Colonel George A. Custer and the Seventh Cavalry, Coolidge was arguably more open to learning about the actual political, economic, and social circumstances that prevented American Indians from being full members of American society than his Oval Office predecessors.

Coolidge, President Warren G. Harding's vice president, assumed the presidency when Harding died in office on August 2, 1923. After serving out the remainder of Harding's term, Coolidge twice ran successfully for reelection, serving from 1923 to 1929. His presidencies coincided with a decade of profound transformation in American society. Before the Wall Street crash of 1929, the rapid pace of modernization (the introduction of radio, the automobile, the telephone, aviation, and the power grid) and the economic prosperity rippling throughout the country yielded the expression "Coolidge prosperity." Americans Indians, however, did not share in the general well-being. When more than twelve thousand American Indian servicemen returned home from World War I, they felt the devastating repercussions of two nineteenth-century government policies that still tragically affected American Indian lives: the allotment of Indian lands and forced assimilation into mainstream society.

Although military and government officials (and civilians who felt they could speak for Indians) strenuously debated questions about whether American Indians could be subject to the draft and integrated into the military, most Americans never knew that American Indians' service in World War I was remarkably high in proportion to their percentage of the population. Coolidge, however, knew. During his first year as president, Coolidge personally signed the certificates sent to Native nations across the country expressing the United States' gratitude for their "willing sacrifices" and the "bravery of their sons in the military and naval service of the United States" (Britten [1997] 1999, 160). On June 2, 1924, Coolidge signed the Indian Citizenship Act, which granted U.S. citizenship to all American Indians who were not already citizens, notably those who fought in World War I.

Coolidge's administration also appointed the Committee of One Hundred, a national advisory reform panel established to evaluate federal institutions and programs dealing with Indian nations. The most important outcome of the committee was the recommendation that the government conduct an in-depth investigation into life on reservations. In response, Coolidge's secretary of the interior, Hubert Work, requested in 1926 that the Institute for Government Research (now the Brookings Institution) conduct the assessment. Completed in 1928, the investigation resulted in the groundbreaking volume *The Problem of Indian Administration*, also known as the Meriam Report. The report called for a complete overhaul of U.S. federal Indian policy (Lamar 1996, 174).

Coolidge was not known for being a great reformer in any aspect of his presidency, nor is he regarded as such where American Indians are concerned. As a rule, Coolidge was recognized for exercising executive restraint and relying heavily on cabinet members and administrators to carry out the government's business (Miller Center for Public Affairs 2016). Coolidge's Oval Office predecessors during the late nineteenth century had shifted responsibility for Indian affairs to the secretary of the interior and cut back on receiving American Indian delegations (Viola 1981, 111). Coolidge himself made few changes in federal Indian policy. He is most severely criticized for doing nothing to stop the devastating consequences of the General Allotment (Dawes) Act of 1887. But Coolidge, who did not flinch from appearing ridiculous by posing in an eagle-feather headdress, also did not flinch from shining a light on the widespread, deplorable conditions of reservation life. With the publication in 1928 of the Meriam Report, succeeding administrations would begin to introduce incremental reforms that supported American Indian political authority and cease their all-out assault on Native cultural and spiritual practices.

President Franklin D. Roosevelt is inducted into the Boy Scout Order of the Arrow, 1933. Ten Mile River Camp, New York. Times World Wide Photo. Courtesy of the Franklin D. Roosevelt Library and Museum, Hyde Park, New York

WHEN PRESIDENT ROOSEVELT WAS INDUCTED into the Boy Scouts of America's Order of the Arrow on August 23, 1933, a photograph of the event was widely disseminated. Already stricken by polio and having lost the use of his legs, Roosevelt is seated in the back of his open presidential car, nicknamed the Sunshine Special. He wears an Order of the Arrow sash across his chest and, on his head, a Plains Indian–style feather headdress. (Film footage of the newsworthy event shows a cheerful Roosevelt asking if the headdress is on straight.) An Order of the Arrow scout, or Arrowman, dressed in a fringed Indian costume and wearing his own feather headdress, presents Roosevelt with a model tipi. Founded in 1915, Order of the Arrow remains a nationwide organization within the Boy Scouts of America (BSA), whose members dress in Indian costumes to induct their newest Arrowmen around a bonfire. Besides being an exemplary scout, the inductee is also one who has distinguished himself by his devotion to scout camping traditions and environmental stewardship (Boy Scouts of America 2016).

First as the governor of New York State and then as the president of the United States, Franklin D. Roosevelt staunchly supported the Boy Scouts. Roosevelt served as president of the Greater New York Council of the Boy Scouts of America in 1924 and 1927. He was instrumental in securing approximately sixteen thousand acres of land in the Catskills to create the Ten Mile River Camp for New York City Boy Scouts. Then the largest of any Boy Scout camps, it is where Roosevelt was inducted into the Order of the Arrow.

Two important early twentieth-century predecessors of the Boy Scouts were the League of Woodcraft Indians, established in 1902 by Ernest Thompson Seton, and the Sons of Daniel Boone, established in 1905 by Daniel Carter Beard. Both groups associated manliness with what many sensed, if not feared, was a bygone way of life in America. With the closing of the western frontier and dramatic population shifts from farms to cities, many felt that modern urban life simply did not equip boys with the challenges and skills they needed to become men. In short, they feared boys were growing up without the pioneer spirit that theretofore had defined the American character (see page 124). Seton and Beard, both of whom would help establish the Boy Scouts of America, agreed that outdoor life and wilderness experiences were key to instilling physical and moral fortitude, as well as qualities of self-reliance and independence.

Seton and Beard had, however, one profound and irreconcilable disagreement. Seton felt that American Indians provided a positive, even crucial, model for the young. To him, an essentially outdoor organization naturally should model itself after American Indian societies (it should include, for example, tribes, chiefs, and keepers of wampum), not unlike counterpart organizations for adults such as the Improved Order of Red Men or the Tammany Society (see pages 86 and 90). Seton strongly believed that American Indian customs and traditions dovetailed perfectly with the ideals of scouting.

Beard felt Seton's ideas were preposterous, wrongheaded, and un-American. Beard argued his position so vociferously that Seton left the Scouts in 1916. But in the long run he was not able to dampen scouts' powerful attraction to "living Indian-style in the woods" (Deloria 1998, 120). In time, large segments of American society—including the U.S. military, which, owing to Native contributions during World War I, had come to acknowledge American Indians as not only "distinctly American" but also "real Americans"—no longer shared Beard's intense biases against Indians. By 1932, when Roosevelt became president of the United States, the Seton–Beard dispute was far in past. Beginning in 1940 in New York State, Seneca anthropologist and Indian progressive Arthur C. Parker succeeded in establishing a Boy Scout program that trained American Indian youths to serve as camp counselors, to provide at least the possibility of some genuine intercultural understanding (Deloria 1998, 125).

When Roosevelt entered the White House, the entire country was gripped by the Great Depression, a crisis that threatened the very stability of American life. Roosevelt saw the Boy Scouts as a means of safeguarding the country's social fabric. After his induction into the Order of the Arrow, he described to the assembled scouts the Civilian Conservation Corps (CCC), his recently established New Deal program for restoring prosperity to the country by offering work to young unmarried men (*New York Times* 1933b, 17). Wearing his Order of the Arrow sash, he stated that the CCC was for the most part modeled on the Boy Scouts. They are both based, Roosevelt said, on the same fundamentals (ibid.).

Like the fraternal patriotic organizations that date to the American revolutionary generation (see pages 50, 86, and 90), the Boy Scouts has long associated many of its core values (manliness, self-reliance, and loyalty) with American Indians. Its members draped themselves—and, on at least one occasion, a willing U.S. president—in American Indian imagery to symbolize those essential principles. At a time when early twentieth-century modernization, industrialization, and urbanization had left Americans unsure of their lives, they found succor in what they held to be the fundamentals of American Indian societies.

THE INDIAN-HEAD NICKEL, also known as the Buffalo nickel for the image of an American bison on its reverse, was minted from 1913 until 1938 and remains one of the best-loved American coins. James Earle Fraser, the French-trained American considered to be one of the United States' leading sculptors of public monuments throughout the first half of the twentieth century, designed both sides of the iconic coin in 1912 (Bowers 2007, 33). Fraser's sculptures of individuals captured not only the likeness but also the intellect, temperament, status, and historical importance of his subjects. Additionally, his works were allegorical and expressed a symbolic idea. For sites in Washington, DC, Fraser created the bronze monument to Alexander Hamilton, 1923, outside the Treasury Building; the winged-horse statuary group, *Arts of Peace,* 1930, at the entrance of Memorial Bridge; and the stone statues *Heritage* and *Guardianship*, 1935, in front of the National Archives. For New York City, he created the bronze equestrian statue of Theodore Roosevelt, 1939, outside the American Museum of Natural History. Other than for the Indian-head nickel, Fraser is probably best known today for his bronze sculpture *End of the Trail*, 1918, which is now at the National Cowboy & Western Heritage Museum in Oklahoma City; Fraser created different versions, which are in assorted collections. While some believe that *End of the Trail* is sympathetic to American Indians, other see in it a weary, dejected Indian who, like the character Chingachgook in James Fenimore Cooper's historical novel *Last of the Mohicans* (1826), is a man without a future, leaving the stage of history.

The time Fraser spent growing up in Minnesota and the Dakota Territory (present-day South Dakota) during the waning years of the frontier made an indelible impression on him. His personal memories of frontier life worked their way into several of his sculptures. Perhaps for this reason, many are surprised that Fraser's highly realistic Indian-head portrait on the nickel coin is not an individual American Indian's profile. Rather, it is a composite image based on the profiles of three Native men: Iron Tail (Oglala Lakota), Two Moons (Cheyenne), and John Big Tree (Kiowa) (Lange 1992, 5). Like James B. Longacre, who designed the three-dollar gold coin of 1854–89, and

James Earle Fraser (1876–1953), designer. Indian-head nickel, 1913; minted 1935. Stamped copper and nickel. Courtesy of the Numismatic Guaranty Corporation, Sarasota, Florida

President Theodore Roosevelt, who commissioned a half-eagle gold coin with an image of Liberty (pages 78 and 102), Fraser wanted to "do something totally American—that is, he wanted to make a coin that could not be mistaken for any other country's coin." Fraser explained his artistic decision: "My purpose was not to make a portrait, but a type" (Bowers 2007, 38–39).

Fraser's initial idea for the nickel's design was to depict an American bison, which would be complemented by a portrait of an American Indian. Tellingly, Fraser's buffalo was based on one he saw in New York City's Bronx Park Zoo, which in 1915 would be sold and slaughtered (Lange 1992, 6). In Fraser's words, the Indian and the buffalo belonged to "our western background"; his obituary relegates the images to the "old West" (*New York Times* 1953b, 28). Essentially, there is no differentiation between the buffalo and Indian-head images engraved on the nickel; symbolically, they reinforce each other. Neither veers into sentimentality. Fraser's American Indian, struck in metal, could no more progress into the future than could the buffalo, hunted to near extinction in the nineteenth century save for an unhappy few lingering in big-city zoos.

Fraser's Indian head is a profoundly memorable image and, like the realistic image of the American bison, deeply familiar to Americans. With the appearance in 1913 of the Indian-head/Buffalo nickel, each of the images became an even more powerful, iconic emblem of America's past. Thought to be no longer encumbered by contemporary issues, American Indians were assigned a timelessness that was, in the minds of many Americans, simply their "natural" state. Considered as an official government commission, the Indian-head portrait, alongside the inscription Liberty, is an extraordinary image.

AS PART OF A NATIONWIDE CAMPAIGN to monumentalize American history artistically, if not ideologically, the U.S. Treasury Department in 1935 invited artists to compete for the opportunity to paint murals for post offices throughout the country. The murals commissioned for post offices—federal buildings that the public visited frequently—could typically measure ten feet high and twenty-five feet wide. Among the winners of the contest to paint murals in the Wichita, Kansas, post office was the Atchison-born artist J. Ward Lockwood. During the 1930s, Lockwood painted Works Progress Administration murals in Taos, New Mexico; Lexington, Kentucky; Washington, DC; and Edinburg and Hamilton, Texas (Eldredge, Schimmel, and Truettner 1986, 201; Lockwood 1940, 268–69). Lockwood was schooled in art at University of Kansas, Lawrence; the Pennsylvania Academy of the Fine Arts, Philadelphia; and in Paris (Eldredge, Schimmel, and Truettner 1986, 201). He had fought in France during the war and had been awarded the Croix de Guerre (Haley, Loran, and Pepper 1964). After the war, he returned to France, set up a studio in the Montmartre in Paris, and studied art there at the Académie Ranson. He soon found, however, that he preferred to study paintings on his own at the Musée du Louvre. After eighteen months in Paris, Lockwood returned to the United States, eventually moving to Taos, New Mexico, where he painted from 1928 until 1939.

Pioneers in Kansas, the oil-on-canvas mural he painted for the first-floor lobby of the Wichita Courthouse, is a nostalgic view of the perseverance of white pioneers. It is a pastiche of stock frontier images: a stagecoach, a steam locomotive, an old-timer, and an Indian taking aim at an iconic cowboy figure on horseback, who returns fire. The pioneer spirit is thrown into clear relief against these "realities" of frontier life. No adversity is great enough to impede them, not even the pioneers' main antagonist, the crouching Indian lying in wait.

Pioneers in Kansas presents a vision of a determined America whose interests (westward expansion) and values (grit, determination, and unwavering faith) are perfectly aligned. It is an homage to a past that Americans in the 1930s believed should never be forgotten—and would never be if Americans remained interested in their own history. When Lockwood painted *Pioneers in Kansas*, America's pioneer days seemed destined to remain a subject of personal and national pride. That the West was not exactly a terror-free zone for American Indians was not one of the painting's messages or a concern of most Americans.

Lockwood explored the painting styles of several different modernist movements, including expressionism, cubism, surrealism, and constructivism (Lockwood 1940, 269, 272). Despite his artistic ease in these styles (usually executed in watercolors), his *Pioneers in Kansas* belongs to the social realism school of painting associated with Federal Art Project (FAP) works of the 1920s, '30s, and '40s, often defined, aesthetically speaking, as antimodernist. Like many FAP paintings, the

J. Ward Lockwood (1894–1963). *Pioneers in Kansas,* **1935.** Oil on canvas. Treasury Building, Wichita, Kansas. Photo by Carol M. Highsmith. Courtesy of the Library of Congress Prints and Photographs Division

mural is an epic history of the American heartland executed in deep, bold colors and with great bravura. But while Lockwood's painting shares much thematically and stylistically with the American social realism movement, it has unique anteced-ents and affinities.

His antecedents are, in part, the late-nineteenth-century, four-color Wild West posters advertising the theatrical spectacles of frontier life that had been eagerly consumed by Americans throughout the 1880s and 1890s. In many ways, *Pioneers in Kansas*'s deepest affinities are with Western films that were Hollywood staples during the first half of the twentieth century. It shared with these films a desire to present a golden age in which ordinary white Americans could see themselves. That longing lasted into the second half of the twentieth century, when a new wave of historians and counterculture filmmakers began to explore an American frontier that was far more complex, gritty, brutal, and amoral. Directly and indirectly, they called into question the country's relationship with American Indians in light of its previously unwavering belief that westward expansion was an American birthright. Films took as their target the mythic representation of "the West" and "the Indian."[1] In short order, paintings commissioned by the U.S. Treasury Department in the 1930s, such as Lockwood's *Pioneers in Kansas*, came to represent a period in American history when historians had not yet begun to critically examine westward expansionism.

IN 1936, WHEN THE U.S. Department of the Interior opened its new building in Washington, DC (known since 2010 as the Stewart Lee Udall Department of the Interior Building), the structure was touted as a "symbol of a new day" (U.S. Department of the Interior 2016). A massive seven-story building that occupies two city blocks, the Department of the Interior's new headquarters was the first Public Works Administration (PWA) building constructed in Washington, DC, during President Franklin D. Roosevelt's presidency. Harold L. Ickes, then the secretary of the interior, commissioned artists (also as part of the PWA program) to paint more than fifty murals on the walls of its vast corridors. Six of the artists were American Indians, one of whom was the now-renowned Chiricahua Apache artist Allan Houser. Houser painted three murals in the building, including *Breaking Camp during Wartime*.

Houser was a prolific painter and sculptor who was influenced by European modernists (such as Henry Moore, Constantin Brancusi, and Jean Arp) as well as his own cultural background. He worked in narrative and abstract styles with an impressive array of media: pencil, charcoal, pastel, ink, watercolor, tempera, oil, marble, alabaster, limestone, steatite, and bronze. He strived in his art to present Apache people with humanity, which for him was a deep, unsentimental reality.

Allan Houser (Chiricahua Apache, 1914–1994). ***Breaking Camp during Wartime, 1938.*** Oil on plaster. Stewart Lee Udall Department of the Interior Building, Washington, DC. Photo by Alex Jamison for the National Museum of the American Indian, Smithsonian Institution, Washington, DC

Houser was Warm Springs Chiricahua Apache. Since the early 1850s, when American soldiers and settlers had first entered the Southwest, they had considered the Apache peoples they encountered there to be "untutored," "heathenish," and the "most untamed of all the races" (Cremony [1868] 1983, 250, 264). Although Apaches were defending their homelands, Americans saw them as "wanderers in the public domain" of the United States (ibid., 312). For the next three decades, on-and-off conflicts as well as raids and counter-raids included acts of brutality on both sides. Apaches and Americans made attempts to achieve peace, but peace for the Americans meant that the Apaches would have to submit to being confined to reservations (Sweeney 2010). In 1886, the U.S. Army removed the Chiricahua Apaches from the Southwest and held them as prisoners-of-war until 1913. Houser's father was one of those removed with the famed leaders Naiche and Geronimo. His mother was born in captivity at Mount Vernon Arsenal and Barracks in Alabama. Houser was born in 1914, just after the Chiricahua were released from their imprisonment at Fort Sill, Oklahoma, and he was raised on stories of relatives who had endured great hardship.

Houser was only twenty-four years old but already recognized as a gifted artist when he received the commission to paint murals in the Department of the Interior. The building houses the Bureau of Indian Affairs, the federal agency that, together with the army, had dictated Chiricahua Apaches' daily lives, including those of Houser's parents, for more than a quarter century while they were held as prisoners of war. Houser's painting *Breaking Camp during Wartime* conveys the dignity of his people, which few white people recognized during the second half of the nineteenth century. Naturally, Houser did not paint "marauders" or "wanderers in the public domain." Poignantly, he chose to paint a scene from the period before the Chiricahua were forcibly removed from the Southwest—that is, when they were fleeing the U.S. Army. This period defined and overshadowed Chiricahua lives for decades and is captured in Houser's scene: a father and mother with their infant in flight.

The subject is not unknown in Western art history. The Holy Family's flight into Egypt had been a well-established biblical theme in European art at least since the early fourteenth century, when the master Renaissance artist Giotto painted Mary and Joseph's journey with the Christ child. In Houser's mural, the Chiricahua Apache family is moving swiftly but serenely through their domain—a sacred landscape. It is minimally but fully defined by the familiar plants of traditional lands, including the seasonal cycle of the mesquite that distinguishes the Chiricahua's territory and here suggests the family's movement through that territory.[1] More important, their sacred domain is signified by the holy being in the sky who watches over them. With its location on the walls of the Department of the Interior Building in Washington, DC, and its eloquent depiction of the Chiricahua world, *Breaking Camp during Wartime* proves as subversive as Allan Houser was gifted.

Allan Houser (Chiricahua Apache, 1914–1994).
Breaking Camp during Wartime, **1938** (detail). Oil on plaster. Depictions of familiar plants including the seasonal cycle of the mesquite that distinguishes the Chiricahua's territory.

IN 1939, THE FEDERAL ARTS PROJECT, part of the Works Progress Administration (WPA), commissioned a series of eight posters to advertise the exhibition *Indian Court* displayed in the United States pavilion at the Golden Gate International Exposition in 1939. René d'Harnoncourt, who was then an administrator for the Indian Arts and Crafts Board at the U.S. Department of the Interior, and Frederic H. Douglas, a longtime curator at the Denver Art Museum who was one of the first in the art world to champion American Indian forms of visual expression, jointly curated the exhibition. D'Harnoncourt hired California painter Louis Siegriest to design the posters for the exhibition after having seen a poster Siegriest had designed that featured an American Indian basket motif (Siegriest 1975). Significantly, the d'Harnoncourt-and-Douglas-curated exhibition at the Golden Gate International Exposition occurred just as the country and its cultural institutions were beginning to organize events showcasing American Indian art. It was followed in 1941 by the exhibition *Indian Art of the United States*, which d'Harnoncourt and Douglas also curated, at the prestigious Museum of Modern Art in New York City. These two exhibitions were pathbreaking for a number of reasons.

First, in the early-to-mid-twentieth century, modernist artists and intellectuals, to whom Louis Siegriest was attuned, were among the first to recognize and appreciate American Indian forms of artistic expression, at least on a stylistic level. They regarded "tribal arts" as superb examples of pure and uninhibited artistic expression in the sense that the techniques involved in making them were not dictated by a stifling European academy (see Maurer 1984). It is true that early modernist artists are more widely known for their interest in indigenous African artistic expression, but many of them—Enrico Donati, Max Ernst, Adolph Gottlieb, Paul Klee, Pierre Matisse, Wolfgang Paalen, Isabelle Waldberg—also were drawn to American Indian visual expression, for which they felt artistic as well as intellectual and emotional affinity. Before modernists' attention to it, the Western world had largely seen American Indian visual arts—paintings, sculptures, ceramics, or textiles—as relics, curios, or (even worse) ethnographic specimens. It was modern artists' tastes and aesthetic sensibilities that created an appreciation of American Indian artistic expression in big-city cultural institutions in the United States.

A second reason d'Harnoncourt and Douglas's two exhibitions were trailblazing is that while surrealists and other modern artists were being drawn to American Indian forms of visual expression, Americans in the early twentieth century were generally turning away from the European influences that had dominated American cultural life during the Gilded Age. They were growing increasingly conscious of their own cultural traditions, or lack thereof, and were beginning to appreciate the deep time span represented by American Indian arts. In the early twentieth century, some scholars, arts administrators, and art dealers began to describe Native art as part of America's ancient and noteworthy cultural heritage.

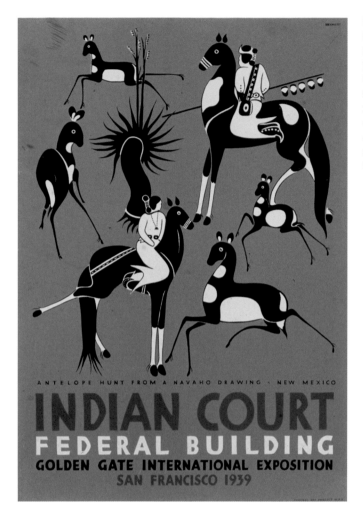

Louis Siegriest (1899–1985) after Ha-So-De (Narciso Platero Abeyta [Diné], 1918–1998). Golden Gate International Exposition poster, 1939. Silkscreened print. Courtesy of the Library of Congress Prints and Photographs Division, WPA Poster Collection

American Indian art was starting to provide Americans in certain circles with a deeply desired artistic pedigree.

A third contributing factor to the somewhat sudden appreciation of American Indian arts in the United States was the appointment of John Collier as the commissioner for the Bureau of Indian Affairs. Collier was a social reformer and advocate for American Indians. He sought to reverse the longstanding federal policy of forced assimilation. In sharp contrast to his predecessors, Collier supported American Indians in their efforts to sustain their cultural and artistic traditions (see McLerran [2009] 2012). It was Collier who had established the American Indian Arts and Crafts Board to promote and preserve American Indian art forms.

Attuned to the artistic currents of his day, Siegriest closely identified with modernist artists who sought artistic freedom in their own work, explored indigenous styles, and in so doing played a key role in redefining dismissive attitudes toward American Indian art. When Siegriest set out to design eight posters for the Golden Gate International Exposition, he looked to the artwork produced by contemporary American Indian artists at the Studio School, which art instructor Dorothy Dunn had launched as part of the Santa Fe Indian School. Siegriest was clearly captivated by the powerful draftsmanship of Diné artist Ha-So-De (Narciso Platero Abeyta), whose artwork is distinguished by a strong graphic style and intense expressiveness. The silkscreened equestrian and antelope figures in Siegriest's 1939 poster are adapted from Ha-So-De's 1936 painting *Antelope Hunt*. Ha-So-De often organized such figures, for which he was especially well known, around a yucca plant, as Siegriest also did in the poster. However, while the location of Ha-So-De's painting is unknown, it is safe to assume that the poster reproduces figurative elements from the painting and not the entire work. Siegriest's apparent readiness to take such liberties suggests a certain lack of professional regard for Native artists.[1]

The Golden Gate Exposition and Siegriest's striking posters occurred at a time when the United States was beginning to officially promote American Indians' artistic heritage as part of the nation's own. While this was a far cry from perceiving American Indian expressive forms as crudely made curios and relics, it also presented a new problem that would vex American Indians and U.S. museums throughout the twentieth century, namely, the appropriate stewardship of objects of cultural patrimony, including sacred objects, that were alienated from the American Indian societies that had created them.

American Indian forms of visual expression were long regarded as having been anonymously produced. Perhaps this explains why neither Ha-So-De nor any of the other American Indian artists whose work provided the arresting graphic power of the Federal Arts Project posters were acknowledged or credited. While d'Harnoncourt, Douglas, and Siegriest were ahead of their time in recognizing the aesthetic force of American Indian contemporary art, the country's awakening art world was decades away from recognizing that Western concepts of art and aesthetics often clash with American Indians' beliefs about their cultural patrimony housed in museums.

LOCATED NEAR THE ENTRANCE to Arlington National Cemetery, the U.S. Marine Corps War Memorial commemorates all members of the Marine Corps who have died defending the United States since 1775. Created by Austrian-born American sculptor Felix de Weldon, it renders in bronze one of the most familiar, if not the most frequently reproduced, photographic images from any American war. More than five times life-size, it captures a dramatic and seminal moment in one of the deadliest battles of World War II and connects Americans to the marines who fought in that war, and by extension all American wars.

The genesis of the composition and character of the memorial sculpture is the Pulitzer Prize–winning black-and-white photograph taken by Associated Press photographer Joe Rosenthal of six servicemen raising a U.S. flag on the island of Iwo Jima on February 23, 1945.[1] The sculpture conveys well the intensity of the physical exertion it took to raise the flag atop Mount Suribachi, the highest peak on the eight-square-mile island, located in an archipelago south of Japan. On the day the flag was raised, the island was still controlled by the Japanese Imperial Army. While de Weldon's sculpture accentuates the concerted efforts of the six servicemen, its intent and focus are concentrated entirely on the powerful symbolism of their objective. Within a month, war-weary Americans would know that the objective was achieved at a devastating human cost. The thirty-six-day Battle of Iwo Jima, which began with the invasion of the island on February 19, 1945, and continued to March 27, 1945, has gone down in history as some of the fiercest and bloodiest fighting in World War II: 5,931 marines lost their lives and 17,372 were wounded (Chapman Jr., 1970, 3; Nalty and Crawford 1995, 21).[2]

When Rosenthal's photograph of the U.S. flag raising at Iwo Jima was released in the United States just two days after it was taken, none of the servicemen were identified (Marling and Wetenhall 1991, 67–73). But the country became transfixed by the image, which was published on the front page of newspapers nationwide. It captured what could only be regarded as a hugely significant, emotionally charged moment in an otherwise horrific battle—and the American public wanted to know who the men were. They read the photograph as "a sign of imminent American victory in the Pacific" (ibid., 73). The marine on the far left of Rosenthal's photo, and de Weldon's memorial sculpture, is Ira Hamilton Hayes, a Private First Class and Akimel O'odham (Pima). Born on the Gila River Indian Reservation in Arizona, Hayes enlisted in the marines in 1942. His company, Company E, Twenty-Eighth Marine Regiment of the Fifth Marine Division, was one of the first to land on Iwo Jima. Five days into heavy combat, five marines (including Hayes) and a navy corpsman were ordered to raise the American flag atop Mount Suribachi.[3] Three of the six would die in the battle. President Roosevelt ordered the survivors home, and they were hailed as national war heroes.

Back in the United States, the flag raisers were pressed into service to help sell war bonds for the U.S. Treasury Department on six multi city tours. When they visited Boston, Houston, and New York, they attracted crowds in the hundreds of thousands. Onlookers always wanted to know which one was Ira Hayes, the American Indian. During the flag raisers' visit to the White House, President Harry S. Truman told Hayes that he was a war hero. Hayes replied, "How can I feel like a hero when 250 of my buddies hit the beach with me and only twenty-seven of us walked off alive?" (Bradley 2002, 264). When the U.S. Marine Corps (Iwo Jima) War Memorial was officially dedicated by President Dwight D. Eisenhower on November 10, 1954, Hayes was present.

Yet Hayes did not enjoy being a war hero, much less a celebrity. He did not even want to be named as one of the flag raisers when the clamor came from back home for the six to be identified (ibid., 268). Nonetheless, Hayes participated in the war-bond drive, which raised an incredible $26.3 billion (Bradley 2002, 268). He also modeled for de Weldon's sculpture (*New York Times* 1954, 26; Marling and Wetenhall 1991, 17, 90, 159). But Hayes remained uncomfortable being the focus of attention wherever he went. Even while he was on his reservation, non-Native people tracked him down, to meet the American Indian who had raised the flag at Iwo Jima. At a time when health professionals in the United States had not yet identified symptoms suffered by combat veterans as post-traumatic stress disorder, Hayes was haunted by the staggering number of marines from his division and company who had died on Iwo Jima. In a way that was uniquely challenging for American Indian combat veterans, Hayes had difficulty reintegrating into civilian circumstances, on and off the reservation. Despite his efforts, Hayes never adjusted to postwar life or his celebrity status. He died in 1955, just months after the dedication of the Iwo Jima War Memorial, at the age of thirty-two.[4]

The U.S. Marine Corps War Memorial is an American cultural icon. Devoid of either allegorical or abstract imagery, it is a commemorative sculpture in the tradition of grand war monuments of the past. Stylistically, de Weldon strove for and achieved heroic realism. He based his facial portraits, including that of Ira Hayes, on life studies (*New York Times* 1954, 26; Marling and Wetenhall 1991, 17, 148). Still, few visitors to the monument today know even that the figure on the far left, reaching toward the flag, represents an American Indian, let alone Private First Class Ira Hamilton Hayes from the Gila River Indian Reservation. When the flag was raised atop Mount Suribachi, it could be seen from everywhere on the island and, by all accounts, every marine and navy corpsman involved with the flag raising immediately appreciated its profound symbolic significance. Surely Ira Hayes shared in the euphoria, however fleeting, before the carnage once again closed in, and the Battle of Iwo Jima raged on for another thirty-one days.

Felix de Weldon (1907–2003). U.S. Marine Corps War Memorial (Iwo Jima Memorial), 1954.
Cast bronze. Courtesy of Richard Tadman/Alamy Stock Photo

IN ADDITION TO USING IMAGERY of Americans Indians throughout its history on medals, monuments, stamps, coins, and structures, the United States also has been using Native terms as well as the names of Native nations and individual American Indians on its military weapons, naval vessels, and aircraft for a surprisingly long time, at least since the Civil War. This remarkable phenomenon speaks to the entangled and conflicted history that American Indians and the United States share. It remains a little-known fact that a significant number of American Indians served as auxiliary federal troops and scouts from the Revolutionary War through the Civil War, and that Indian scouts were first enlisted in the U.S. Army in 1866, remaining in service until the early twentieth century (Department of Veterans Affairs 2012, 4). It was during the twentieth century that the U.S. military's tradition of naming weapons after American Indians began in earnest, as did its tradition of using American Indian imagery in its insignias. One of the most important weapons to be named after a Native nation was a high-velocity, rocket-powered missile.

The five-inch Zuni Folding-Fin Aircraft Rocket was a rocket-powered missile that the U.S. Navy approved for production in 1957. It was created as an improved version of the High Velocity Aircraft Rocket, an air-to-surface missile developed during World War II and used extensively at that time as well as in the Korean War. The air-to-surface and air-to-air Zuni missile had far greater velocity, more penetrating power, and a longer range than the High Velocity Rocket. Its fins folded when not in use to allow efficient carriage in multitube launch pods, and it allowed the use of different types of warheads and fuses. Although the circumstances surrounding its name are shrouded, it may be considered the first of the modern-day advanced weapon systems named after an American Indian tribe.

The Zuni, or more properly A:shiwi, live in present-day New Mexico. They were the first indigenous peoples encountered by the Spanish explorer Francisco Vázquez de Coronado in the present-day American Southwest. In 1539, Estevan, an enslaved Moorish man in Coronado's advance scouting party, happened upon Hawikku, an A:shiwi farming village and regional crossroads for trade and knowledge. One year later, Coronado led his expedition from Mexico north in search of Cibola, the fabled Seven Cities of Gold. Reaching Hawikku, he established a Spanish presence in A:shiwi territory that lasted 140 years. A:shiwi resisted attempts at cultural and political domination (Enote 2010, 134). The Spanish were particularly brutal to the A:shiwi and other Pueblo peoples, which resulted in the Pueblos' driving Spanish soldiers, missionaries, and settlers out of the Southwest in 1680.

By 1957, when the Zuni missile was named, the U.S. military had long been valorizing American Indians for their "warrior spirit." More consequential, the military by then associated American Indians' defense of their homelands and ways of life with its own defense of U.S. national borders and interests; it identified with American Indians on a level that defined who and what it was at its core.

An Mk 16 Zuni Folding-Fin Aircraft Rocket is launched by a U.S. Marine Corps Douglas A-4M Skyhawk, 1957. China Lake, California. Courtesy of the Robert Lawson Photograph Collection, National Naval Aviation Museum, Pensacola, Florida

Throughout the second half of the twentieth century, the U.S. military named other advanced weapons systems after American Indians, including the 1976 Tomahawk subsonic cruise missile. Since the 1960s, military helicopters have also been named after American Indian tribes (see page 144). Interestingly, in 1961 the army named a helicopter after the Lakota (they called it Sioux), a people with whom the U.S. military shared a violent and deadly history throughout the second half of the nineteenth century. On one level, there is clearly much irony in the naming of U.S. military weapons and aircraft after American Indians. Still, the U.S. Department of Defense now acknowledges that American Indians have served in the military from the Revolutionary War to the present. The military also recognizes the many contributions of American Indians, well known and not, such as the code talkers— including A:shiwi code talkers—who served during World War II (see page 154). Yet, although the U.S. military asserts its desire to honor American Indians, the now-more-than-a-century-old naming tradition remains controversial, certainly for many American Indian scholars and activists. For them, it perpetuates a reductionist view of American Indians while masking a painful history.

WHILE CAMPAIGNING in June 1960 to become the Republican nominee for president of the United States, Vice President Richard M. Nixon made a three state swing through the Midwest. While in North Dakota, he made a campaign stop at Minot, about an hour outside the Fort Berthold Reservation, home to the Mandan, Hidatsa, and Arikara, who have been known since 1934 as the Three Affiliated Tribes. Nixon shared the stage with the respected former tribal chairman, Carl Whitman Jr. (Mandan/Hidatsa). In 1960, the former chairman had already served two of his three terms as tribal leader (1948–50, 1956–58, and 1962–64). In what could easily be considered a perplexing show of solidarity, Nixon and Whitman were photographed shaking hands and wearing eagle-feather headdresses—perplexing in light of recent painful events that took place on the Fort Berthold Reservation.

Seven years before Vice President Nixon's visit, the Three Affiliated Tribes had been gravely affected by the construction of the Garrison Dam on the Missouri River. Completed in 1953, the dam is the fifth-largest earthen dam in the world. Dam design and construction are the most complex engineering feats sponsored by any government. Throughout the world, the promise of hydroelectricity or flood control, considered essential to support growing populations, causes ecological damage on a massive scale. Additionally, dam construction all too often disregards indigenous peoples' land rights. The U.S. Congress authorized construction of the Garrison Dam when it passed the Flood Control Act in late 1944. The authorization generated intense opposition from the Three Affiliated Tribes, who lobbied against the dam for ten years. When the Army Corps of Engineers threatened to confiscate tribal lands by right of eminent domain, tribal leaders traveled to Washington, DC, to protest in person (Lawson 2009, 53). They succeeded in temporarily halting the dam project by demanding that Congress acknowledge their treaty rights, which stipulated that land could not be taken from them without their consent or without compensation.

Eventually, under relentless state and federal pressure, the Three Affiliated Tribes agreed to sell 155,000 acres of their land to the U.S. government. In the 1880s, the tribes' land base equaled 12.5 million acres. But as the *New York Times* reported in 1952, "Through the years the white man has nibbled away at the reservation. A few years ago it was down to 600,000 acres. Now they are to lose another 155,000 acres." The dam's reservoir flooded an amazing 95 percent of the tribe's rich bottomlands, including roads, the hospital, the telephone exchange, and the Indian Agency, all of which forced tribal families to relocate (Berman 1988, 57; *New York Times* 1952, 27).

Nixon lost the 1961 presidential election to John F. Kennedy but ran again in 1968, winning his bid for the presidency and serving in office until August 1974. As is well known, Nixon's presidency was deeply stained by his handling of the Vietnam conflict and the Watergate scandal, and the result was his resignation. But too

Vice President Richard M. Nixon meets with the former chairman of the Three Affiliated Tribes Carl Whitman Jr. (Mandan/Hidatsa) 1960. Minot, North Dakota. Courtesy of the Richard Nixon Presidential Library and Museum (National Archives and Records Administration), Yorba Linda, California

often overlooked is the fact that Nixon's five years in the White House coincided with American Indians' fight for self-determination—that is, for tribes' ability to assert and protect their sovereignty and control over their natural resources.

While Nixon's predecessor, President Lyndon B. Johnson, helped open the door to tribal self-determination, it is President Nixon who was responsible for putting an end to the decades-old federal Indian policy of termination—the withdrawing of all federal ties to, and support for, tribal governments, including the removal of Indian lands from federally protected trust status (Hoxie 1996b, 625). Nixon also restored Indian lands to tribes and oversaw what was arguably the most pro-Indian administration in the twentieth century (Johnson 2012). Years of protracted conflicts and paternalistic policies toward American Indians had resulted in grave infringements on American Indians' human rights. During his administration,

President Nixon reshaped the direction of national policy toward American Indians and brought about changes that were foundational to tribal self-governance (Lawson 2009, 243).

Forging personal relationships has always been integral to Native diplomacy—including diplomacy that might lead to mutual coexistence with the United States. Carl Whitman Jr. was a seasoned tribal chairman who had a concrete understanding of the congressional and judicial branches of the U.S. government owing to his tribe's lengthy effort to lobby against the flooding of tribal lands and its subsequent efforts to ensure that the tribe would be justly compensated for its land, which was eventually flooded in order to create the Garrison Dam. Whitman's genial handshake with Vice President Nixon is probably best understood as both a sincere gesture and the action of an adept tribal leader who recognized the importance of always working to strengthen federal regard and support for tribal sovereignty. Nixon as president recognized, understood, and supported that goal by providing crucial building blocks. He began by establishing a working group, composed of key high-level government officials and respected American Indian leaders, charged with recommending major Indian policy proposals that would be important steps leading to tribal self-determination.

OKLAHOMA'S PLACE IN U.S. HISTORY is without parallel. Perhaps this explains the curious *Unity*, a bas-relief adorning the U.S. Federal Building and Courthouse built in Oklahoma City in 1961. The facility's architect was Oklahoman Dow Gumerson, whose design for the building has been described as a classic example of new formalism. In keeping with that minimalist aesthetic, it is largely devoid of architectural ornament, the emphasis being on purity of design and high-quality construction materials (Indiana limestone and granite). The *Unity* bas-relief is one of two relief sculptures placed unobtrusively above two side entrances to the building.[1] Seen from below, they barely project from the building's façade.

Unity was designed by Bernard Emerson Frazier, a sculptor admired regionally for his public commissions in Missouri, Oklahoma, and his native Kansas, and for his own modernist aesthetic, which complemented Gumerson's. Frazier had a predilection for incorporating personifications in his public works; his relief on the Oklahoma City courthouse represents Unity as a woman whose flowing hair seems to symbolically unite a pilgrim (or homesteader?) couple to her right and an American Indian couple to her left. The two American Indians are defined by the slightest suggestion of a feather headdress and breechcloth worn by the man. Their faces turn away from Unity and the pilgrims. The pilgrims are identified by the small details of the woman's coif, or head covering, and by the missal she holds in her right hand. Their faces similarly turn away from Unity and the Indians. Unity averts her gaze from the Indians, although her left hand enigmatically extends toward them. The couples on the *Unity* relief are a strange juxtaposition. Despite the name of the work, they convey no sense of amicability.

The meaning of the relief must be understood against the backdrop of Oklahoma's unique history. In 1907, Oklahoma became the forty-sixth state to join the union. The land designated for the state was essentially the same territory Congress had set aside in 1828 as the destination to which the U.S. government would remove eastern American Indians, thereby opening up to white settlement almost all southern land east of the Mississippi. Indian Territory, as it become known, was never controlled by a federally appointed governor; it was an Indian-occupied region of the United States that was not part of any organized territory or state, and it was essentially governed by American Indians (Bailey and Bailey 1996, 271). The federal practice of removing Native nations from their homelands and resettling their entire populations in Indian Territory began in earnest in 1830 with the passage of the Indian Removal Act. The removals occurred in several phases through 1894, when Chiricahua Apaches (removed from Arizona in 1886 and held at U.S. military installations in Florida and Alabama), were again moved to Fort Sill, outside Lawton, Oklahoma (see page 128). More than twenty-five Native nations ultimately were uprooted from their homelands by the federal government and removed to Indian Territory.

Bernard Emerson Frazier (1906–1976). *Unity,* **1966.** Limestone. U.S. Federal Building and Courthouse, Oklahoma City. Photo by Carol M. Highsmith. Courtesy of the Library of Congress Prints and Photographs Division

In 1885, with the country having long since expanded all the way to the Pacific and settlement having spread throughout the continental United States, the government declared large portions of Indian Territory open to non-Indians. That year, the government sponsored the first of several land sales in Indian Territory, and waves of Americans flooded in to stake their claims. The biggest land rush in what is now Oklahoma—and the biggest in U.S. history—occurred in 1893. During the same decade, Congress created the powerful Dawes Commission and, under terms set down by that commission and the General Allotment Act of 1887, broke up the previously communally held lands that had been designated for Native nations; the lands were allotted as small parcels to individual tribal members. All remaining land was classified as "surplus" and opened up for non-Indian settlement (Bailey and Bailey 1996, 273).

Frazier's relief is a minimalist work on a federal courthouse designed with a minimalist aesthetic. Still, in addition to its location on a building that symbolizes the American republic in a state that was rushed into existence—and that forced Native peoples to yet again give up their tribal lands to homesteaders—the relief is rich in symbolic detail. The relief seems best understood as a meditation on the past that addresses the United States' rapid settlement of Indian Territory and tries to awaken consciousness of unity between two symbolic couples, who appear as remote from each other as they are mute.

Boeing AH-64E Apache Longbow helicopter, Arizona, 2014. © The Boeing Company

THE U.S. ARMY FIRST TOOK DELIVERY of the AH-64 Apache helicopter in 1984. The Apache and its upgraded variants have been designed to be fast, highly maneuverable, heavily armed, and devastatingly powerful military attack aircraft. Most of the systems that protect its crew and vital systems have backups. Apaches are considered the most advanced and toughest attack helicopters in the world, and their pilots, who are required to maneuver these complex, eight-ton aircraft, are part of an army elite.

It is ironic that the U.S. Army named the most powerful helicopter in the world Apache, given the U.S. military's long and difficult history fighting Apache Indians. On February 24, 1863, the United States designated as a new territory the traditional homelands of Apache peoples, to be called Arizona Territory. It soon became a place where settlers, drifters, prospectors, surveyors, investors, geologists, soldiers, Mexicans, several different Apache tribes, several other Native peoples, and others collided. In 1871, nearly 150 White Mountain Apaches—mostly women and children—were killed in a predawn attack by a "combined party of Americans, Mexicans, and Tohono O'odham" (Jacoby 2008, 2). The massacre was so shocking to Easterners that they demanded a criminal trial, but Arizona Territory would be engaged in conflict for the next quarter century.

In an effort to stem the violence, U.S. Army general George G. Crook declared that any Apaches not living on four hastily established reservations were "hostiles," or enemy combatants. Consequently, skirmishes between certain Apaches and the army became a feature of life in a territory rapidly filling with military posts; towns; stagecoach lines; railroads; telegraph lines; ranches; and major copper, silver, gold, and lead mines. The number of Apaches refusing to be confined to reservations actually was small. Still, judging from articles published in the territorial newspapers, it is not surprising that an author would one day write, "Apache! The word struck terror in the hearts of generations of White frontiersmen in northern New Spain and the Southwestern United States" (Dobyns 1971, 1). By the mid-1880s, the U.S. Army's central purpose was to capture Apaches not already confined to reservations in Arizona Territory.

Army soldiers stationed at military posts in Arizona Territory considered Apache Indians' ability to maneuver throughout the terrain superior to theirs. Famously, the army depended on Apache scouts to find and fight "hostile" Apaches, most notably the Chiricahua leaders Geronimo and Naiche and their followers. Throughout the last quarter of the nineteenth century, army officers wrote article after article in military journals about their involvement in what they called the Apache Campaign (Britton 1885; Elliott 1910; Clay 1929; Parker 1929).

On September 9, 1983, almost a century after the Apache Campaign in Arizona Territory was concluded, the world's most powerful attack helicopter was unveiled at its Mesa, Arizona, production site. At that dedication ceremony and those of subsequent generations of Apache helicopters, White Mountain Apache tribal officials have been present. The U.S. Army maintains that its tradition of naming an aircraft after American Indian nations is a tribute to those tribes. "The name," it explains, "should appeal to the imagination without sacrifice of dignity, and should suggest an aggressive spirit and confidence in the capabilities of the aircraft. The name should also suggest mobility, agility, flexibility, firepower, and endurance" (U.S. Army Publishing Directorate 2014, 8, 9). White Mountain Apache leaders have repeatedly expressed their pride in having the most powerful attack helicopters named after their people and having the strength and history of their tribe recognized around the world (Baha-Walker 2007, 4, 19). In recalling his participation at a dedication ceremony, long-time tribal chairman Ronnie Lupe told his people, "It was an honor to be asked ... to conduct a blessing ceremony for the new ... Apache helicopter. My prayers were humbling and down to earth just like the Medicine man who prayed for me before and after my time in Korea. When the time comes for survival, it's good not to be seen; it's important to be strong, ready, and focused; and it's vital to return home. Within these parameters, I asked the Creator for help" (Lupe 2013, 3, 5). On another occasion, Lupe explained, "At dawn, we began the day with the warrior blessing, for the WAH-64 Apache Longbow. It is our way, for a warrior to be prepared to respond quickly and decisively. This blessing is given to allow man and machine to come close as possible to perform and function as one, so that all military pilots of the Longbow Apache will return from battle, with their mission complete" (Lupe 1998, 2).

It is a puzzle to many that the army would seek a symbolic association with American Indians, and perhaps more so that many American Indians tribes accommodate them. Especially in recent decades, American Indians have served in the U.S. armed services at a higher rate in proportion to their population than all other American demographic groups. They lend their name, or image, on terms that they themselves find meaningful. According to one White Mountain official, in the case of the Apache helicopter, doing so is a reminder to the world of Apache history and the Apaches' ongoing place in it.

White Mountain Apache tribal chairman Ronnie Lupe (middle) gives the traditional Apache sacred blessing to the first Apache Block III aircraft, 2011. With him are Ramon Riley (left) and Jerry Gloshay Jr. (right). Photo by Sofia Bledsoe. Courtesy of Defense Video Imagery Distribution System

IN ONE SENSE, THE STORY of Jim Thorpe (Sac and Fox) begins the same way as many others in American sports: "A kid born on a farm . . ." But then it diverges. The farm where Thorpe was born was in Indian Territory—present-day Oklahoma, the land to which the U.S. government in 1830 had removed American Indian nations from "vast tracts of wilderness" that it desired to make available for white settlement. In 1869, the government removed the Sac and Fox nations to Indian Territory from what became the state of Kansas (Thorpe 1981, 99). By 1887, when Thorpe was born outside the small town of Prague, the U.S. government had again opened up Sac and Fox land for settlement (see page 141). Ultimately, the Sac and Fox land base in Indian Territory was reduced to its present one thousand acres. Out of this history of uprootedness and dislocation, Jim Thorpe burst onto the world stage in 1912 at the Olympic Games in Stockholm, became the greatest football running back of his era as well as a professional baseball player, and appeared twice as a national symbol on U.S. postage stamps, first in 1984 and again in 1998.

For a small, two-dimensional image, the compositional layout on the 1998 postage stamp is highly effective. The painterly rendition of Thorpe's shoulders, head, and face impart sculptural weight and volume to the athlete. The tonal variations in his face especially build up monumentality. The pole-vaulting scene silhouetted against the flat white of Thorpe's T-shirt, combined with the flatness of the stamp's background colors, captures the headiness of Thorpe's triumphant appearance at the Stockholm Olympics and hints at the wonder of the larger-than-life athletic accomplishments to come. While the pole-vaulting scene does the work of creating the greater compositional structure of the small stamp, the effect of the radiant yet somber palette imparts a subtle but definite psychological quality to Thorpe's portrait.

If U.S. postage stamps are intended to tell national stories, the *Jim Thorpe* thirty-two-cent stamp tells a tumultuous one, rooted deeply in American history. If they are intended to capture what American life was like at a given point in time, the stamp captures a uniquely American experience that, paradoxically, few Americans really know. Thorpe was named James Francis Thorpe on all official papers, and Wa Tha Huck (Bright Path) by his mother, who died while Thorpe was at boarding school. At the age of six, he was sent to the Sauk and Fox Mission School, then to Haskell Indian Junior College in Lawrence, Kansas and finally to Carlisle Indian Industrial School in Pennsylvania. The boarding schools were intended to help prepare young American Indians for living in mainstream American society. They were established purposely to take Native children away from their parents, communities, and any tribal influences social reformers believed would hinder them from living in the twentieth century.

Famously, Jim Thorpe's athletic career began at Carlisle when he caught the eye of the legendary football coach "Pop" Warner. Thorpe went on to become a top

Jim Thorpe **thirty-two-cent stamp, 1998.** Ink on paper. © 1998 United States Postal Service. All rights reserved. Used with permission. Jim Thorpe™ is a registered trademark of the Estate of Jim Thorpe

performer in track and football, repeatedly leading the Carlisle football team to victories. He left Carlisle to play two seasons of minor league baseball but returned in 1911 to advance the football team to national fame; he was named an All-American that year, and again in 1912. At the 1912 Olympics, Thorpe became the first athlete to win gold medals in both the pentathlon and decathlon. Less than a month later, though, Thorpe's gold medals were rescinded when it was deemed that he had violated his amateur status by playing professional baseball. The medals were restored posthumously, in 1982, with an apology by the International Olympic Committee. Between 1913 and 1919, Thorpe played professional baseball for the New York Giants, Cincinnati Reds, and Boston Braves, and between 1915 and 1930, he played with seven professional football teams, beginning with the Canton Bulldogs. Thorpe was the first president of the American Professional Football Association (since renamed the National Football League). In 1950, an Associated Press poll of sports writers and broadcasters called him the "greatest male athlete of the half-century" (*New York Times* 1950, 142).

In Thorpe's American sports story, his Indian-ness was an ever-present factor; he was often referred to in the press as the "Indian athlete" or the "famous Indian athlete." Yet on the field, to Thorpe, being Sac and Fox was secondary to his athleticism. Off the field, according to Grace, Thorpe's daughter and a prominent advocate for American Indian causes, her father never forgot that he was an Indian (Thorpe 1996, 627). Thorpe was an athlete, not a political activist. But his political consciousness was awakened before he left boarding school. He was born into a generation of American Indians shaped by their boarding school experiences and, contrary to the intentions of those boarding schools, grew up knowing that he was and always would be Indian and different. Thorpe internalized this contradiction and, through it, saw himself in the continuum of American Indian history. His life on and off the field was too rough and tumble for him to be caught up in the romanticism of his own athletic success. Thorpe opposed government paternalism, interference in tribal affairs, and American Indians' status as "wards of the nation" (Wheeler 1979, 196, 204). He knew how many American Indian men fought for the United States in World War I and wanted them recognized as American citizens (see page 117). He was equally mindful that land had been taken from Native nations "whenever the government wants land" (ibid., 204).

Together with a small legion of more vocal and intellectually minded American Indian professionals who entered the nation's public arena in the first half of the twentieth century, Jim Thorpe took an assertive stance against the United States' paternalistic Indian policies (Wheeler 1979, 196). The portrait masterfully executed in shades of ocher on his 1998 postage stamp and enriched by the inclusion of a seminal feat from his early career, portrays a man of many outstanding accomplishments in his chosen field. Interestingly, the number of stamps the U.S. Postal Service issued to honor accomplished American Indians in the twentieth century is very few. Thorpe is but one of three.[1]

ORIGINALLY MINTED IN 2000, the Sacagawea one-dollar coin represents the first time in U.S. history that the likeness of an actual American Indian, man or woman, has appeared on a circulating U.S. coin. The decision to use an image of Sacagawea was based on a recommendation made by a committee of prominent Americans— including a member of Congress, the president of the American Numismatic Society, and an under secretary of the Smithsonian Intuition—that was charged to evaluate suggestions from the public for "a woman from history" to grace a new U.S. dollar coin. Sacagawea was the "ultimate dark horse candidate" (Clines 2000). The committee, chaired by the U.S. Mint director, Philip N. Diehl, recommended that dark horse—the young Shoshone woman who from April 7, 1805, to August 17, 1806, accompanied President Thomas Jefferson's Corps of Discovery expedition on their famed overland route through the part of Native North America that had been claimed by France. In 1803, France sold that territory to the United States in the land deal known as the Louisiana Purchase. With the Louisiana Purchase, the United States acquired approximately 827,000 square miles, doubled its size, and put the country well onto the path of becoming a continental power, an aspiration that Jefferson held dear (Meacham 2013, 410).

The artists who submitted proposals for the image of Sacagawea to be engraved on the dollar coin were instructed to be "sensitive to cultural authenticity" (U.S. Mint 2016b). New Mexico sculptor Glenna Goodacre created the winning design, which depicts Sacagawea carrying her infant son, Jean Bapiste, on her back; Thomas D. Rogers Sr. designed the reverse side of the coin. Sacagawea, shown in three-quarter profile (a departure from numismatic tradition), looks straight at the coin's holder. Her portrait was based on that of Randy 'L He-dow Teton, a young Shoshone-Ban-nock/Cree from the Fort Hall Reservation in southeastern Idaho. Clearly, Goodacre was sensitive to Sacagawea's age, facial features, and, not insignificantly, the fact that Sacagawea undertook the arduous journey while caring for an infant child.

The young Shoshone woman named Sacagawea is thought to have been about seventeen years old when she agreed to travel with the corps to interpret for Captains Meriwether Lewis and William Clark. She accompanied them as they moved west from Fort Mandan in present-day North Dakota across Shoshone territory to the Pacific Ocean and back. To the expedition, Shoshone territory was the "unknown" or "uncharted West"—or, in Lewis's words, a country on which "the foot of civilized man had never trodden" (quoted in Ambrose 1996, 212).

Jefferson's Corps of Discovery has been described as the "most momentous expedition in American history" and the "first American epic" (McMurtry 2001). Jefferson instructed Lewis and Clark to pay attention to rivers, specifically to find the source of the Missouri River and to map the principal waterways to the Pacific Ocean "for the purposes of commerce" (Hoxie 2007, 1). Lewis (Jefferson's former personal secretary) and Clark were told to keep extensive journals and to announce to the indigenous peoples they encountered that their territories had been taken over. Jefferson told the explorers to tell the Missouri, Otoe, Lakota, Arikara, Mandan, Hidatsa, Assiniboine, Blackfeet, Shoshone, Nez Perce, and numerous other Native nations that "henceforth we become their fathers and friends, and that we shall endeavor that they shall have no cause to lament the change" (Jefferson quoted in Jackson 1978, 166). Jefferson's mission was hardly focused on establishing genuine diplomatic relations between Native nations and the United States. It was to focus in no small measure, however, on learning about the Indian peoples who were encountered (Hoxie 2007, 8). Jefferson instructed Lewis and Clark to conduct ethnographic studies, and he provided them with a list of questions so they could gather and record specific types of information (Ronda 1984, 113). Their studies—based upon interviews, observations, collecting, and occasional participation in tribal activities—were naturally limited by linguistic challenges (ibid., 115), as were any diplomatic overtures.

After Lewis and Clark's triumphant return and report to Jefferson, Sacagawea was virtually forgotten until the expedition's centennial observances. At that time, Sacagawea emerged as "something of a national heroine" and, together with Lewis and Clark, entered the myth of the American West (Lurie 1985, 32). Among the journals of Lewis and Clark's transcontinental expedition, references to Sacagawea are infrequent. She is usually referred to only as the Indian woman, Charbono's Indian wife, or sometimes the Squaw or Janey, the nickname she was given by the corps (McMurtry 2001). The "unknown" West was, of course, heavily populated with Native nations. Lewis and Clark's expedition encountered nearly fifty of them, yet virtually all references to individual Native peoples in the expedition journals are exasperatingly brief.

Remarkably, little is known of Sacagawea's life (Gilman 2003, 118). Unfortunately, her story cannot even be discerned piecemeal in the journals. Yet she is sufficiently discernable in them for the reader to want to know more about her character, thoughts, emotions, and needs. Enough of her presence drifts through the journals for this young Shoshone woman to have become part of our national memory. On the *Sacagawea* dollar coin, her depiction is not conflated iconographically with the personification of Liberty, nor is she depicted wearing a feather headdress (see page 78). She is a young Shoshone woman—not the Indian woman, not Charbono's Indian wife, not the Squaw, nor Janey, but Sacagawea, who took part in an arduous journey that looms large in the American imagination. The journey's consequences for Native peoples are being examined through readings of the expedition's journals that seek to understand more deeply the complexity of the interactions between the corps and Native peoples—how they tried, or not, to comprehend each other, what accommodations they attempted to make, the ways in which they misunderstood each other—as the United States endeavored to "master a continent" (Gilman 2003; Hoxie 2007; Howe and Tallbear 2006; Meacham 2013 410; Ronda 1984).

Glenna Goodacre (b. 1939), designer. *Sacagawea* **one-dollar coin, 2000.** Stamped copper alloy. United States *Sacagawea* one-dollar coin images courtesy of the United States Mint, Washington, DC. Used with permission. *Sacagawea* one-dollar coin obverse ™ 1999 United States Mint, Washington, DC

U.S. Congressional Gold Medals, Code Talkers Recognition Act of 2008, 2013.

Medal awarded by the Code Talkers Recognition Act of 2008 to the Cherokee Nation for its service in World Wars I and II. Obverse: designer Donna Weaver, engraver Michael Gaudioso; reverse: designer and engraver Joseph Menna.

CONGRESSIONAL GOLD MEDALS, together with the Presidential Medal of Freedom, are the highest civilian honors that the U.S. government can bestow upon an individual in appreciation for his or her distinguished achievements or contributions to the country. The earliest Congressional Gold Medals were awarded to individuals who distinguished themselves during the American Revolutionary War. George Washington was the first recipient, as were six other individuals who fought in the American Revolution. Ironically, American Indians were depicted on two of those early congressional medals,[1] but an American Indian was not awarded a medal until 2000, when twenty-nine Navajo veterans of World War II received Congressional Gold Medals for their service as code talkers.

Thirteen years later, the country recognized the many other American Indian military veterans who had also served as code talkers. While American Indians have fought alongside non-Native Americans since before the Revolutionary War, their military contributions, including those of World War I and World War II code talkers, have gone largely unacknowledged. During the world wars, American Indians were called upon to use their fluency in both English and their Native languages. For the latter, orthographies and dictionaries, which would have aided military enemies, often did not exist. The bilingual Native servicemen relayed intelligence critical to military operations, such as troop movements, casualty reports, and supply needs. At times in code and always in their tribal languages, their messages were used to subvert the German army in World War I and Italian, German, and Japanese forces in World War II. Throughout the twentieth century, however, the overwhelming majority of American Indian veterans were subjected to various forms of discrimination when they returned to civilian life, despite their service in foreign conflicts. In the Jim Crow South, they often were categorized as "persons of color."

Medal awarded by the Code Talkers Recognition Act of 2008 to the Cheyenne River Sioux Tribe for its service in World Wars I and II. Obverse: designer Donna Weaver, engraver Michael Gaudioso; reverse: designer Don Everhart, engraver Jim Licaretz.

Medal awarded by the Code Talkers Recognition Act of 2008 to the Choctaw Nation for its service in World Wars I and II. Obverse: designer Thomas Cleveland, engraver Phebe Hemphill; reverse: designer Don Everhart, engraver Jim Licaretz.

Medal awarded by the Code Talkers Recognition Act of 2008 to the Fond du Lac Band of Lake Superior Chippewa Tribe for its service in World War II. Obverse: designer Donna Weaver, engraver Michael Gaudioso; reverse: designer Donna Weaver, engraver Charles L. Vickers.

Medal awarded by the Code Talkers Recognition Act of 2008 to the Fort Peck Assiniboine and Sioux Tribes for their service in World War II. Obverse: designer and engraver Don Everhart; reverse: designer Joel Iskowitz, engraver Jim Licaretz.

To bestow the honor of a Congressional Gold Medal, two-thirds (290) of the members of the House of Representatives must cosponsor legislation for the purpose. On October 25, 2008, the 110th Congress passed the Code Talkers Recognition Act (Public Law 110-420), which requires that medals be issued in recognition of American Indian code talkers. The act states, "The service of Native American code talkers to the United States deserves immediate recognition for their dedication and valor; and honoring of Native American code talkers is long overdue."

The designs of the U.S. congressional code talker gold medals present a striking contrast to the stagnant image of the near-naked American Indian wearing a plumed skirt and stand-up feather headdress that endured for three centuries (see pages 27, 32, 66), and to the frozen-in-time image of the Plains Indian warrior that associated Native peoples with the past and came to represent all American Indians (see pages 102 and 108), thus masking their diversity and evolving identities. Each code talker medal illustrates with clarity and cultural specificity an American Indian tribal member engaged in relaying military intelligence. On the reverse of each medal is an image meaningful to the individual and tribe being honored.

On November 20, 2013, the U.S. government formally recognized thirty-three American Indian nations for the dedication and valor of their tribal members who served as code talkers in the U.S. armed services during World Wars I and II (see pages 110 and 137). The ceremony honoring the code talkers took place in Emancipation Hall at the U.S. Capitol. President Barack Obama and members of Congress presided. Poignantly, House Speaker John Boehner said in his opening remarks, "Today we meet to immortalize men who we are, in a way, meeting for the first time." Twenty-five surviving code talkers were present to be recognized for their valor and personally honored with a U.S. Congressional Gold Medal.

Medal awarded by the Code Talkers Recognition Act of 2008 to the Ho-Chunk Nation for its service in World War II. Obverse: designer and engraver Michael Gaudioso; reverse: designer and engraver Don Everhart.

Medal awarded by the Code Talkers Recognition Act of 2008 to the Hopi Tribe for its service in World War II. Obverse: designer Joel Iskowitz, engraver Don Everhart; reverse: designer Joel Iskowitz, engraver Renata Gordon.

THE WEST ENTRANCE DOORS to the Library of Congress's John Adams Building are handsome glass-paneled doors created in 2013 that fittingly pay homage to the history of the written word. The John Adams Building is named after the second president of the United States who, on April 24, 1800, signed the law establishing a library for the U.S. Congress (Allen 2014).[1] The west entry glass doors faithfully and elegantly reinterpret the original bronze doors created for the building when it first opened to the public in 1939.

Lee Lawrie, a renowned architectural sculptor, designed the bronze doors. Each set of doors incorporates high-relief figures of six mythical and human individuals who, "since ancient times, have been credited with giving the art of writing to their peoples" (Scanlon 2009). When in recent years the Lawrie bronze doors were found to no longer meet building codes, the Architect of the Capitol decided to leave the historic doors permanently open and to have new, glass-paneled doors placed just inside the originals. The figures on the new doors, which meticulously mirror those originally sculpted in bronze, were cast out of glass, then etched and hand rubbed to get the desired surface and translucency (Fireart Glass 2017).

On the center set of doors, the bronze and glass versions feature a figure of Sequoyah, a Cherokee silversmith who is the only person known to world history to have singlehandedly devised a written language without first being literate in a language (King and Chapman 1993, 41).[2] Presumably to match the other figures, he is depicted in vaguely ancient Egyptian garb. He holds his syllabary in his right hand and a pipe in his left.

Over a period of twelve years, Sequoyah (also known as George Guess) determined that the Cherokee language consisted of eighty-seven distinct sounds, and he created a symbol for each of them. Sequoyah made his syllabary public in 1821; within a year, thousands of Cherokees had become literate (ibid., 40). Missionaries and Cherokees quickly translated the Bible, prayer books, and hymnals into Cherokee.

Sequoyah's syllabary also allowed Cherokees to publish a bilingual tribal newspaper, *The Cherokee Phoenix*, first issued in February 1828, a tumultuous year in United States and Cherokee history. A vigorous national debate concerning the possible removal of southeastern Indian nations, including the Cherokee Nation, from what was then almost half of the United States consumed the country. The debate focused on whether this action befitted a new republic devoted to Enlightenment principles.

The anachronistic attire in which Sequoyah is represented on the Library of Congress doors removes him entirely from the turbulent Cherokee–U.S. history in which his syllabary played a significant role. Unlike a small circle of elite Cherokee statesmen of his time who wore Western suits, Sequoyah, as depicted in 1838 in a colored lithograph (originally published in *History of the Indian Tribes of North America …* by Thomas McKenney and James Hall), wore a colorful calico frock

Washington Glass Studio and Fireart Glass. *Sequoyah,* **2013.** Cast glass. John Adams Building, Library of Congress, Washington, DC. Photo by Jamie Coughlin. Courtesy of Fireart Glass

over a white cotton trade shirt with a cravat, and a turban made from imported fabric. He also smoked a clay pipe, not the Plains Indian–style pipe with a stone bowl and wooden stem he is shown holding on the Library of Congress doors. Though not visible in the lithograph, Sequoyah would have also worn a Cherokee-made, finger-woven wool sash around his waist, baldrics, woolen leggings, and beaded deerhide moccasins that might have been lined with silk. Far from evoking mythic or ancient times, the clothing Sequoyah actually wore reflected Cherokee engagement with nineteenth-century global commodity trade. More than that, it echoed the high-stakes geopolitics of his day, in which Cherokee leaders were struggling to retain control of their territory as well as their social and political lives.

A small circle of Cherokees fluent in English—statesmen, ministers, plantation owners, and the editors of the *Cherokee Phoenix*—placed themselves at the center of the national debate raging over their possible removal from their homelands. Like the Founding Fathers and other great thinkers who shaped the United States during the early republic, Cherokee leaders were prolific writers in many forms: letters, essays, critiques, sermons, editorials, petitions, pamphlets, and speeches. They corresponded privately with intellectuals of the day, published carefully reasoned arguments against removal in national newspapers such as the *Niles' Register*, and submitted written petitions to the U.S. Congress arguing against their threatened removal. They wrote in the English alphabet and Cherokee syllabary.

The Cherokee leaders published bilingual articles, editorials, and sharp critiques of political dishonesty in the *Cherokee Phoenix*, made possible by Sequoyah's unparalleled invention, so that their positions concerning the question of removal could be read by both their people and Americans. They kept their fellow Cherokee and Americans informed of the latest threats to Cherokee liberty, including the increasing assaults of white squatters, unwanted appearances of U.S. government surveyors inventorying their tillable lands and springs, and the controversial and shameful acts (e.g., refusing to allow Cherokees to congregate) perpetrated against their people by state and federal governments (Davis 1979, 132, 135).

In 1835, the state of Georgia seized the printing press of the *Cherokee Phoenix*, an act that denied Cherokees one of the cornerstones of democracy: a free press (Davis 1979, 144). Literacy and their carefully reasoned position papers against removal ultimately did not help the Cherokees. The U.S. government deemed the Cherokees, like other Native nations, best placed beyond the settled borders of the United States. It is ironic and fitting that Sequoyah, whose "fame rests entirely upon his intellectual achievement" (Fogelson 1996, 580) of inventing a syllabary that enabled members of the Cherokee Nation to become literate virtually overnight, should be twice so handsomely and meticulously enshrined on doors of the Library of Congress. His oddly anachronistic attire makes it easier to disregard the complex and controversial events surrounding his extraordinary invention.

AFTERWORD

PAUL CHAAT SMITH

HERE'S WHAT WE ALWAYS FORGET: the United States is the strangest and unlikeliest country in the history of Earth.

Fortunately, a fellow named Nassim Nicholas Taleb explains why. Well, not why the United States is strange and unlikely, but the question of why we forget. Taleb invented the Black Swan theory. It describes outlier events as having three characteristics. First, they are so unthinkable no one sees them coming. Second, after taking place, they have extraordinary impact. Basically, something that could never happen does, and that happening changes the world. Third—this is the cool part—human nature instantly begins rationalizing the unthinkable event into something we could have seen coming, not really so shocking or impossible, something that was, in hindsight, actually inevitable.

The two most often cited examples are 1492 and 9/11. To those numbers, I would add the United States itself as right up there with the biggest and blackest of Black Swans.

Let me walk you through this.

Imagine a place and time that never existed.

Fourteen ninety-one: all of the Americas, from the frozen Arctic North to the land of the penguins way down south, the same as it ever was except this: the complete absence of human beings. Nobody lives here. And nobody ever has. And imagine Columbus nevertheless sailing west, just as he did in our world, and the ocean highway he built leading to European settlement, more or less the way we remember it.

In this scenario, all we can be sure of is that almost nothing would have gone down the way it actually did. Because in reality every single place Europeans went, they found people.

On the Atlantic seaboard of the future United States, the English found people. This shaped everything they did. For example, while still in England they prepared for their journey west by studying accounts of Spanish encounters with the Inka and Aztec, in order to create their playbooks for New England and Virginia. They knew that people who were not Spanish or English would be their immediate neighbors, and that lots more would be their distant neighbors. Whether or not they could find that new place called Brazil on a map, the English knew it was already inhabited. People, all over the place.

Now imagine the opposite: realizing that the known world is vastly larger than previously understood, and nobody is home. Empty. So strange. It would be like how some people look at the stars: is anybody out there? I picture Europeans hoping to find people. *Where are they???* It would be so lonely to be in such a vast place. And terrifying. But also, scary to find them. Because how could such a continent, which already seems enormous and grows impossibly larger with every river crossed and mountain range scaled . . . how could it not have human beings somewhere?

And wouldn't it have been boring for Europeans to find only each other? I mean, why take a dangerous trip across the ocean just to be around the same people who annoyed you in high school? Might as well stay home.

Fourteen ninety-two was the biggest event in human history, because it was the moment each half of the world, which had known nothing of the other, realized the other existed. This fact supercharged that moment and everything that followed. Human beings, who had been going about their business for tens of thousands of years, were suddenly confronted with millions of new people. Sure, living far away, but really, not all that far away, just a few months, and before too long just a few weeks. These new people, in what Europeans would soon call the New World, might as well have been from a different universe. It was hard to believe the two hemispheres lived under the same sun, the same moon, and (mostly) the same stars.

Actually, it was more a different timeline than a different universe. Humans have been the same messed-up species for two hundred thousand years. If one thinks of the world in 1500 as a sports league, which one definitely should not, the Eastern Conference had a ten thousand–year head start, with agriculture and superior large mammals, whereas the Western Conference was pretty new, with animals that were cool but not large enough to ride or plow fields. Plus, not everybody wanted to be farmers.

The point is this: inhabited America changed everything. It was the X factor in all that would follow.

As for the preposterousness of the United States, the argument is pretty straightforward. In the space of four lifetimes, a struggling colonial outpost became the richest and most powerful country that ever existed. Some think this was God's will, but it had more to do with luck, timing, perfect geography, and riding the wave of industrial revolutions that created incredible, unprecedented wealth. The United States was also the first nation-state committed to the idea that all human beings have rights, and the first organized in opposition to rule by kings and emperors. It was radical for the time, and pretty far out even today.

Christopher Hitchens, that ferocious critic of the American empire, once, perhaps grudgingly, called the United States the last revolution standing. He was reminding us of all the failures between 1776 and the twenty-first century, from Haiti to the revolutions of France and Russia. They opened with terrific first acts, followed by all manner of catastrophe. For all its horrific flaws and crimes, the American republic is more good than bad, more democratic than most, and still ruled by a constitution that's lasted two centuries.

As Cécile R. Ganteaume notes in the introduction to this book, the American national project was from the very beginning characterized by the fact of these not-European people in every direction the colonists looked. "[The country] has always been preoccupied with defining what is American and has never been able to escape the question of how to practice its professed democratic ideals in its relationship with American Indians."

Ganteaume presents us with a bracing and unexpected argument: the United States has been profoundly shaped from the very beginning by its intricate and complex relationship with American Indians. The images she discusses offer a startling new way to think about the American past, with centuries of tantalizing clues and secrets hiding in plain sight, as they map this complicated negotiation.

They also expose the emptiness and banality of the usual portrayals of Native history as a mournful recitation of inevitable wars lost, land stolen, death, disease, and broken agreements. In tales devoid of drama or surprise, Indians are valiant losers, existing only as obstacles rather easily overcome. The histories read as if written by real estate agents.

An even bigger surprise comes in the second part of Ganteaume's thesis: U.S. policy toward American Indians, often filled with rhetoric of deep concern and compassion, has been shaped with intense awareness of the country as a democratic experiment.

This idea has a spooky resonance in the current moment. Stumbling into the third decade of the twenty-first century, the United States is a battered prize fighter a few years past his prime. The punches not quite so lethal, the footwork just a touch slower. Every fight no longer ends in victory. Everyone can see what's coming. Even so, until that day arrives, he's still the greatest boxer in the game.

The country remains peerless: it remains the planet's oldest democracy, and the only superpower. No other nation can claim those things. But there are problems.

In not very many years, the country turns two hundred and fifty. Even the sturdiest structures start breaking down once you hit the quarter-millennium mark.

The United States faces profound challenges: its international standing is declining (being a superpower isn't what it used to be), sustained economic booms are a distant memory, and democracy itself is a question, to millions a cynical joke. Americans are increasingly divided by culture, education, food, and television: the two coasts, the big cities, and university towns are surrounded by a sea of red. Tens of millions of us seem to loathe each other, and we can't agree on what constitutes a fact.

This is a bigger change than is often acknowledged. Not the part about hating each other, but the living in our curated bubble thing. Just a few generations ago Americans bought their food in the same supermarkets, and watched the same movies and television shows. Even a poor person could dream of owning a Cadillac or having dinner at the finest restaurant in town. There was something very American, very democratic about this. Coca Cola was obviously the world's greatest soft drink, and it was exactly the same product for everyone. There was no special version for the rich.

The economic gaps have grown vast, and so have the cultural divides. It is unlikely there will ever be a pop star who rules the airwaves the way Sinatra and Elvis did in the last century. These kinds of things—Coca Cola, three TV networks, a supermarket being just a supermarket—were part of what defined being an American for a long time. The number of things all Americans share is smaller than it has ever been. We all have smart phones and the Internet, but we experience them in radically individual ways.

And yet, even now, Indians are one of the few symbols in American life that transcend demographics and politics and bubbles. Indians represent authenticity and freedom. Indians represent the country itself. Indians are so embedded in American life that most rarely even think about it. The dream catcher on the rearview mirror and the headdress advertising insurance, carpeting, football teams, or baking powder never require an explanation. They just are. Although Americans rarely talk about it, we ratify the presence of Indians in our pantries, on our money, on the highways, and at stadiums with a silent recognition that yes, this is something right and good that should continue, this somehow makes sense, even though it doesn't, exactly. It's that Black Swan after-the-fact rationalization, when the unthinkable happens and we need to reconstruct it as natural and thinkable after all.

What does it really mean? I choose to be an optimist, and say it means that Americans understand that the country has always been and always will be entangled with and conflicted about Indians.

It's the country saying to Indians, imaginary and real, past and present: without you, there is no us.

Notes

FOREWORD

1. In 2005 the American Psychological Association called for the retirement of all Indian mascots, symbols, and images by sports teams, citing the harmful effects of racial stereotyping, especially on the self-esteem of young people.

INTRODUCTION

The World's Oldest Enduring Republic

1. In his September 15, 2015, interview on the *Charlie Rose Show*, Justice Breyer explained:

Who are we, as Americans? I mean you know, we didn't all descend from King Arthur and we're not all descendants of Charlemagne. Who are we? We are people, in part, who Thomas Jefferson said and the founders said are engaging in an experiment. And when Lincoln is at Gettysburg and Lincoln says, "Four score and seven years ago our forefathers brought forth on this continent a nation conceived in liberty and dedicated to the proposition that all men are created equal." That's what he said, and pointed back to the Declaration of Independence. And he said, "We are engaged in great civil war testing whether that nation, or any nation so conceived and dedicated, can long endure." You see the thought? We are an experiment at the time of the founding—there is no other country engaged in democracy and the protection of human rights trying to govern themselves. At the time of the Civil War, there still isn't one, really, though they're coming along, and we are here as an experiment to see if we can, in fact, "so endure,"

in Lincoln's words. And, indeed we have so far, with plenty of ups and downs, but the experiment is not over.

A View of the Obelisk Erected under Liberty-Tree, 1766

1. Fourteen of the sixteen figures have been identified as the Duke of York, the Marquis of Rockingham, Queen Charlotte, King George III, General Conway, Colonel Barre, William Pitt, Lord Dartmouth, Alderman Beckford, Charles Townshend, Lord George Sackville, Mr. Dennis De Berdt, John Wilkes, and Lord Camden (American Antiquarian Society 2011).

2. A liberty pole is a long wooden pole surmounted by a Phrygian cap—that is, the cap worn by formerly enslaved people in ancient Rome. During colonial times, members of the Sons of Liberty often erected liberty poles in towns as an act of rebellion against what they considered to be tyrannical British rule.

Vignette for the *Royal American Magazine*, 1774

1. Isaiah Thomas, editor of the *Royal American Magazine*, had an enormous personal library to which, presumably, Revere would have had access. Among such descriptions of the calumet and its uses are Jonathan Carver's *Travels through the Interior Parts of North American, in the Years 1767 and 1768*, and Baron de Lahontan's *New Voyages to North America, Vols. A and B*. In Volume A of his book, Lahontan wrote, "The red Calumets are most esteem'd. The Savages make use of 'em for Negotiations and State Affairs, and espe-

cially in Voyages; for when they have a calumet in their hand, they go where they will in safety. ... The calumet ... has the same effect among Savages, that the flag of friendship has amongst us" (Lahontan 1703, 36).

Design proposal for the Great Seal of the United States, 1780

1. The committee members were William Churchill Houston, James Lovell, and John Morin Scott (U.S. Department of State 2003, 2).

Daniel Morgan Congressional Gold Medal, 1790

1. The U.S. Congressional Gold Medal was awarded "in recognition of the 'fortitude and good conduct' displayed by Brigadier General Daniel Morgan, and the officers and men under his command, in the action at Cowpens, in the state of South Carolina on January 17, 1781" (*Journal of the Continental Congress 1774–1789* 19: 246–47, cited in Glassman 2015, 21).

William Penn's Treaty with the Indians, 1682, 1827

1. The three other reliefs are Antonio Capellano's *Preservation of Captain Smith by Pocahontas,* 1825; Enrico Causici's *Landing of the Pilgrims,* 1825; and *Conflict of Daniel Boone and the Indians,* 1826–27.

Baptism of Pocahontas, 1839

1. Captain John Smith, in his publication *Generall Historie of Virginia . . .* (1624), was the first to describe the event, which was thereafter taken as fact for three centuries. In the early twentieth century, scholars began to question whether the event had ever taken place, casting serious doubt for a couple of reasons: Smith did not mention the event in his *True Relation of Such Occurrences and Accidents of Note As Hath Happened in Virginia* (1608) or *Description of New England* (1616), but only in later works; additionally, he claimed that a similar event happened to him in Turkey. Many twentieth- and twenty-first-century scholars have described Smith as a fabulist.

2. Besides the Chapman painting and a scene in the frieze of Pocahontas saving the life of Captain John Smith, three other representations of Pocahontas hang in the U.S. Capitol: a painting modeled after the engraving by Simon van de Passe published in *Bazilioologia: A Booke of Kings . . .* (1618); a sandstone bas-relief by Antonio Capellano from 1825 (also of Pocahon-

tas saving Captain Smith's life), which is located above the west door of the Capitol rotunda; and an oil portrait by an unknown artist, which was presented to the U.S. Senate in 1899 and hangs in the Office of the Secretary of the Senate.

The Death Whoop, 1849–55. Cover of Historical and Statistical Information Respecting the History, Condition, and Prospects of the Indian Tribes of the United States, 1851–57

1. Schoolcraft documented his experiences in his *Personal Memoirs of a Residence of Thirty Years with the Indian Tribes of the American Frontiers* (Philadelphia: Lippincott, Grambo, 1851).

Hiawatha Boat centerpiece, 1871

1. See Clements (1990) for a discussion of Schoolcraft's "textual fidelity" in his transcriptions of Ojibwe oral narratives.

Monument to Forty-Second New York Volunteer Infantry "Tammany" Regiment, 1891

1. It is for this reason that Alexander Hamilton, John Jay, and James Madison wrote *The Federalist Papers* (1788), which were originally published serially as newspaper articles, in which they argued for the ratification of the Constitution proposed by the Continental Congress on September 17, 1787 (see Scigliano 2001).

Indian-head half-eagle gold coin, 1909

1. While eagle-feather headdresses have captured the imagination of Americans, Plains Indian men wore other styles of headdresses that embodied deep cultural meaning as well. See Greene (2015) for a discussion of a different style of headdress that Sitting Bull depicted himself wearing in his ledger art.

2. Plains Indian men still wear eagle-feather headdresses on important ceremonial occasions. Women occasionally publicly don their husband's headdresses.

Dumbarton Bridge Kicking Bear sculpture, 1915

1. Brown had a deep interest in public buildings and urban planning. One of his many prestigious jobs in Washington, DC, was as the historical adviser on a renovation of the White House in 1901–02 (Bushong 2008, 5).

2. In 1890, Kicking Bear made a pilgrimage to the Walker River Reservation in Nevada to meet the Paiute holy man Wovoka. The Ghost Dance rituals and teachings came to Wovoka in a vision when he was sick with a fever (Hittman 1996,

700). According to the revelation, "Indians could restore their lands and recover their deceased ancestors" by performing certain ritual dances and by adhering to certain principles of virtuous and peaceful living (Hoxie, 1996a, 223). When Kicking Bear returned home, he dedicated himself (until prohibited by the U.S. government) to spreading Wovoka's Ghost Dance teachings.

Pioneers in Kansas, 1935

1. Many such works began appearing in the 1960s, but two classics are Arthur Penn's film *Little Big Man* (1970) and Richard Slotkin's book *The Fatal Environment: The Myth of the Frontier in the Age of Industrialization, 1800–1890* (1985).

Breaking Camp during Wartime, 1938

1. Chiricahua Apache artist Oliver Enjady has suggested that the four plants may represent the seasonal cycle of mesquite (personal communication, September 26, 2016). Mesquite beans were an important traditional food for Chiricahua.

Golden Gate International Exposition poster, 1939

1. I am thankful to Bruce Bernstein for calling my attention to this likelihood.

U.S. Marine Corps War Memorial (Iwo Jima Memorial), 1954

1. As is well known, a U.S. flag was raised atop Mount Suribachi twice, and Joe Rosenthal's Pulitzer Prize–winning photograph documented the second flag raising. The first U.S. flag that was raised was a small one; it was replaced with a larger one.

2. These numbers constitute the greatest casualties the U.S. Marine Corps has suffered in any battle. Only 1,083 soldiers of the Japanese Imperial Army's force of twenty thousand men survived the Battle of Iwo Jima (Chapman 1970, 3).

3. The other five flag raisers were Corporal Harlon Block, Private First Class Rene Gagnon, Private First Class Harold Schultz, Private First Class Franklin Sousley, and Sergeant Michael Strank (Office of the U.S. Marine Corps Communication 2016).

4. The unique difficulties American Indian combat veterans faced when returning to civilian life after World War II are explored in N. Scott Momaday's Pulitzer Prize–winning novel *House Made of Dawn* (1968).

Unity, 1966

1. The companion relief to *Unity*, over the opposite entrance to the courthouse, is titled *Destiny*. Also carved by Frazier, it is equally enigmatic. It portrays a man and woman, seen frontally. Their faces, however, are turned to the left. A large eagle, seen in profile, faces right.

Jim Thorpe thirty-two-cent stamp, 1998

1. The other two American Indians honored on U.S. postage stamps for their careers are Cherokee humorist Will Rogers (twice) and dancer and choreographer of American Indian heritage Katherine Dunham. By comparison, the U.S. Postal Service has honored 150 African Americans, thirty-six Jewish Americans, fifteen Italian Americans, and fourteen Hispanic Americans, according to a report compiled in 2003 by the Order Sons of Italy in America.

U.S. Congressional Gold Medals, Code Talkers Recognition Act of 2008, 2013

1. The early congressional medals (technically awarded by the Continental Congress) were given to Major General Anthony Wayne in 1779 and Brigadier General Daniel Morgan (see page 62) in 1790.

Sequoyah, 2013

1. At that time, it was simply called the Annex Building, as it was built to house books that could not be accommodated in the library's main building. It was later called the Thomas Jefferson Building. In 1980, it was yet again renamed, as the John Adams Building.

2. According to a Library of Congress blog, the figures represent Hermes, the messenger of the gods; Odin, the Viking-Germanic god of war and creator of the runic alphabet; Ogma, the Irish god who invented the Gaelic alphabet; Itzama, god of the Maya; Quetzalcoatl, the god of the Aztecs; Sequoyah, an American Indian; Thoth, an Egyptian god; Ts'ang Chieh, the Chinese patron of writing; Nabu, an Akkadian god; Brahma, the Indian god; Cadmus, the Greek sower of dragon's teeth; and Tahmurath, a hero of the ancient Persians (see Cole 2008).

References

Allen, Erin. 2014. "The Library in History: The John Adams Building at 75." Library of Congress blog. April 25. https://blogs.loc.gov/loc/2014/04/the-library-in-history-the-john-adams-building-at-75/.

Allman, William, and Melissa Naulin. 2011. *Something of Splendor: Decorative Arts from the White House.* Washington, DC: White House Historical Association.

Ambrose, Stephen. 1996. *Undaunted Courage: Meriwether Lewis, Thomas Jefferson, and the Opening of the American West.* New York: Simon & Schuster.

American Antiquarian Society. 2011. "The Illustrated Inventory of Paul Revere's Works at the American Antiquarian Society: Revere Collection Box 2." http://www.americanantiquarian.org/Inventories/Revere/b2.htm.

American Civil War Museum. 2016. "Object Record: Guard of the Daughters of Powhatan Flag." Accessed June 2. http://moconfederacy.pastperfectonline.com/webobject/262AD70B-6A88-450C-88E1-677841525251.

Axtell, James. 1992. *Beyond 1492: Encounters in Colonial America.* New York: Oxford University Press.

———. 1997. *The Indians' New South: Culture Change in the Colonial Southeast.* Baton Rouge: Louisiana State University Press.

———. 2001. *Natives and Newcomers: The Cultural Origins of North America*. New York: Oxford University Press.

Babits, Lawrence E. 2001. *A Devil of a Whipping: The Battle of Cowpens.* Chapel Hill: University of North Carolina Press.

Baha-Walker, Margaret. 2007. "From the Office of the Vice Chairwoman Margaret Baha-Walker." *Fort Apache Scout* 46 (15): 4, 19.

Bailey, Garrick and Roberta Glenn Bailey. 1996. "Indian Territory." In *Encyclopedia of North American Indians*, edited by Frederick E. Hoxie, 271–73. Boston: Houghton Mifflin.

Barriero, José. 2015. "Strong in Our Hearts: The Legacy of the Inka Road." In *The Great Inka Road: Engineering an Empire*, edited by Ramiro Matos Mendieta and José Barreiro, 1–10. Washington, DC: National Museum of the American Indian and Smithsonian Books.

Barthes, Roland. (1957) 1972. *Mythologies*. Translated by Annette Lavers. New York: Hill and Wang.

Bassett, Jane, and Peggy Fogelman. 1997. *Looking at European Sculpture: A Guide to Technical Terms.* Los Angeles: J. Paul Getty Museum.

Battistini, Matilde. 2005. *Symbols and Allegories in Art*. Translated by Stephen Sartarelli. Vol. 6 of *A Guide to Imagery*. Los Angeles: J. Paul Getty Museum.

Bergland, Renée. 2000. *The National Uncanny: Indian Ghosts and American Subjects.* Hanover, NH: University Press of New England.

Berkhofer, Robert F., Jr. 1978. *The White Man's Indian: Images of the American Indian from Columbus to the Present*. New York: Alfred A. Knopf.

———. 1988. "White Conceptions of Indians." In *History of Indian-White Relations,* edited by Wilcomb E. Washburn, 522–47. Vol. 4 of *Handbook of North American Indians,* edited by William C. Sturtevant. Washington, DC: Smithsonian Institution.

Berman Terri. 1988. "For the Taking: The Garrison Dam and the Tribal Taking Area." *Cultural Survival* 12 (2).

Bernheimer, Richard. 1952. *Wild Men in the Middle Ages: A Study in Art, Sentiment, and Demonology.* Cambridge, MA: Harvard University Press.

Bewley, Marius. 1965. "America's Heroic Moment." *New York Review of Books.* April 8. http://www.nybooks.com/articles/1965/04/08/americas-heroic-moment/.

Bialostocki, Jan, and Jaroslaw Pelenski. 1980. "Art and Politics: 1770–1830." In *The American and European Revolutions, 1776–1848: Sociopolitical and Ideological Aspects*, edited by Jaroslaw Pelenski, 363–93. Iowa City: University of Iowa Press.

Bieder, Robert E. 1986. *Science Encounters the Indian, 1829–1880: The Early Years of American Ethnology.* Norman: University of Oklahoma Press.

———. 1988. "Non-Indian Biographies: Schoolcraft, Henry Rowe (1793–1864)." In *History of Indian-White Relations*, edited by Wilcomb E. Washburn, 680. Vol. 4 of *Handbook of North American Indians,* edited by William C. Sturtevant. Washington: DC: Smithsonian Institution.

Black, Allida M. 2009. *The First Ladies of the United States of America.* Washington, DC: White House Historical Association.

Boehme, Sarah E., Christian Feest, and Patricia Condon Johnston. 1995. *Seth Eastman: A Portfolio of North American Indians.* Afton, MN: Afton Historical Society Press.

Bowers, Q. David. 2007. *A Guide Book of Buffalo and Jefferson Nickels: Complete Source for History, Grading, and Values.* Atlanta: Whitman Publishing.

Boy Scouts of America. 2016. "The Order of the Arrow, Scouting's National Honor Society." http://www.scouting.org/scoutsource/BoyScouts/OrderoftheArrow.aspx.

Boyd, Julian P., et al., eds. 1952. *The Papers of Thomas Jefferson,* vol. 6. Princeton, NJ: Princeton University Press.

Bradley, James. 2002. "Raising the Flag on Iwo Jima." In *Booknotes: Stories from American History*, compiled by Brian Lamb, 263–68. New York: Penguin Books.

Bradley, James, and Ron Powers. 2000. *Flags of Our Fathers.* New York: Bantam Books.

Breyer, Stephen. 2015. Interview by Charlie Rose, *Charlie Rose Show,* PBS, September 15, 2015. https://charlierose.com/videos/23810.

Brigham, Clarence S. (1954) 1969. *Paul Revere's Engravings.* New York: Atheneum.

Britten, Thomas A. (1997) 1999. *American Indians in World War I: At Home and at War.* Albuquerque: University of New Mexico Press.

Britton, Davis. 1885. "The Difficulties of Indian Warfare." *Army and Navy Journal* 33 (13): 242–44.

Brown, Glenn, and Bedford Brown IV. 1915. "The Q Street Bridge, Washington, D.C." *American Architect* 108 (October 27): 273–79.

Burdette, Roger W. 2007. *Renaissance of American Coinage: 1905–1908.* Great Falls, VA: Seneca Mills Press.

Bushong, William B. 2008. *Glenn Brown and the United States Capitol.* U.S. Government Publishing Office. https://www.gpo.gov/fdsys/pkg/GPO-CDOC-108hdoc240/pdf/GPO-CDOC-108hdoc240-1-7.pdf.

Calitri, Shannon Smith. 2004. "'Give Me Eighty Men': Shattering the Myth of the Fetterman Massacre." *Montana: The Magazine of Western History* 54 (3): 44–59.

Calloway, Colin G. 1999. "The Continuing Revolution in Indian Country." *Native Americans and the Early Republic*, edited by Frederick E. Hoxie, Ronald Hoffman, and Peter J. Albert. Charlottesville: University of Virginia Press.

Campbell, Thomas P. 2003. "A Best Friend in the White House." *Scouting Magazine*, March-April, 2003.

Chapman, L. F., Jr. 1970. *Iwo Jima: Uncommon Valor.* Washington, DC: U.S. Marine Corps, https://babel.hathitrust.org/cgi/pt?id=uc1.b000510441

Child, Brenda J. 1996. "Boarding Schools," In *Encyclopedia of North American Indians*, edited by Frederick E. Hoxie, 78–80. Boston: Houghton Mifflin.

Clarke, Michael, and Deborah Clarke. 2010. *The Concise Oxford Dictionary of Art Terms.* 2nd ed. New York: Oxford University Press.

Clay, Thomas J. 1929. "Some Unwritten Incidents of the Geronimo Campaign." *Proceedings of the Annual Meeting and Dinner of the Order of Indian Wars of the United States.* Washington, DC: Army and Navy Club.

Clements, William M. 1990. "Schoolcraft as Textmaker." *Journal of American Folklore* 101 (408): 177–92.

Clines, Francis X. 2000. "Public Lives: Sharing a Nation's History and Culture, a Coin at a Time." *New York Times*, February 28. https://nyti.ms/2mqdHdU.

Cody, R. L. 2008. "A Footnote in History: WWI Shoulder Patches of the 4th and 5th Marine Brigades." *Leatherneck* (December 2008): 36–37.

Cole, John Y. 2008. "On These Walls: Inscriptions and Quotations in the Buildings of the Library of Congress—The John Adams Building." Library of Congress. https://www.loc.gov/loc/walls/adams.html.

Collins, Shannon. 2014. "Face of Defense: Native American Navy Veteran Paved Way for Women Sailors." U.S. Department of Defense News. https://www.defense.gov/News/Article/Article/603727/face-of-defense-native-american-navy-veteran-paved-way-for-women-sailors.

Cremony, John C. (1868) 1983. *Life among the Apaches*. Lincoln: University of Nebraska Press.

Daniels, Roger. 2015. *Franklin D. Roosevelt: Road to the New Deal, 1882–1939*. Champaign, Illinois: University of Illinois Press.

Davis, Kenneth Penn. 1979. "Chaos in the Indian Country: The Cherokee Nation, 1828–1835." In *The Cherokee Indian Nation: A Troubled History*, edited by Duane H. King. Knoxville: University of Tennessee Press.

Davis, Robert E. 1990. *History of the Improved Order of Red Man and Degree of Pochahontas, 1765–1988*. Waco, TX: Davis Brothers.

Debo, Angie. 1976. *Geronimo: The Man, His Time, His Place*. Norman: University of Oklahoma Press.

DeLorey, Tom. 1985. "Longacre: Unsung Engraver of the U.S. Mint." *The Numismatist* (October): 1970–78.

Deloria, Philip J. 1998. *Playing Indian*. New Haven, CT: Yale University Press.

———. 2004. *Indians in Unexpected Places*. Lawrence: University Press of Kansas.

Deloria, Vine Jr., and Clifford M. Lytle. 1984. *The Nations Within: The Past and Future of American Indian Sovereignty*. New York: Pantheon Press.

Dobyns, Henry F. 1971. *The Apache People*. Phoenix, AZ: Indian Tribal Series.

Dominguez, Steven, and Kenneth E. Kolm. 2005. "Beyond Water Harvesting: A Soil Hydrology Perspective on Traditional Southwestern Agriculture Technology." *American Antiquity* 70 (4): 732–65.

Dunn, Walter Scott, Jr. 2001. *The New Imperial Economy: The British Army and the American Frontier, 1764–1768*. Westport, CT: Praeger.

Eco, Umberto. 1976. *A Theory of Semiotics*. Bloomington: Indiana University Press.

———. 1989. *The Open Work*. Cambridge, MA: Harvard University Press.

Eldredge, Charles, Julie Schimmel, and William H. Truettner, eds. 1986. *Art in New Mexico, 1900–1945: Paths to Taos and Santa Fe*. Washington, DC: National Museum of American Art, Smithsonian Institution.

Elliott, Charles P. 1910. "The Geronimo Campaign of 1885–1886." *Journal of the U.S. Cavalry Association* 21(80): 211–36.

Ellis, Joseph J. 2015. *The Quartet: Orchestrating the Second American Revolution, 1783–1789*. New York: Alfred A. Knopf.

Enote, Jim. 2010. "Ancestral A:shiwi Plate and Candlestick." In *Infinity of Nations: Art and History in the Collections of the National Museum of the American Indian*, edited by Cécile R. Ganteaume, 134. New York and Washington, DC: HarperCollins and the National Museum of the American Indian.

Evans, Suzanne E. 1996. "Voting." In *Encyclopedia of North American Indians*, edited by Frederick E. Hoxie, 658–60. Boston: Houghton Mifflin Company.

Evening Star. 1896. "Big Sioux Here." February 28, 1896, 2.

Falk, Peter Hastings, Audrey Lewis, Georgia Kuchen, and Veronika Roessler, eds. 1999. *Who Was Who in American Art? 1564–1975: 400 Years of Artists in America*. 3 vols. Madison, CT: Sound View Press.

Feest, Christian. 1984. "From North America." In *Primitivism in 20th Century Art: Affinity of the Tribal and the Modern*, edited by William Rubin, 85–98. New York: Museum of Modern Art.

———. 2014. "The People of Calicut: Objects, Texts, and Images in the Age of Proto-Ethnography." *Boletim do Museu Paraense Emílio Goeldi, Ciências Humanas* 9 (2): 287–303. https://dx.doi.org/10.1590/1981-81222014000200003.

Fireart Glass. 2017. "Entry Doors, Library of Congress, John Adams Building." Accessed April 21. http://fireartglass.com/the_library_congress_fabrication.php.

Fischer, David Hackett. 1989. *Albion's Seed: Four British Folkways in America.* New York: Oxford University Press.

———. 1994. *Paul Revere's Ride*. New York: Oxford University Press.

———. 2005. *Liberty and Freedom: A Visual History of America's Founding Ideas*. New York: Oxford University Press.

Fisher, Celia. 2011. *Flowers of the Renaissance*. Los Angeles: J. Paul Getty Museum.

Fleming, E. McClung. 1965. "The American Image as Indian Princess 1765–1783." *Winterthur Portfolio* 2: 65–81.

———. 1967. "From Indian Princess to Greek Goddess, 1783–1815." *Winterthur Portfolio* 3: 37–66.

Fogelson, Raymond. 1996. "Sequoyah." In *Encyclopedia of North American Indians*, edited by Frederick E. Hoxie, 580–82. Boston: Houghton Mifflin Company.

Frankel, Oz. 2000. "Schoolcraft, Henry Rowe (1793–1864)." In *The History of Science in the United States: An Encyclopedia*, edited by Marc Rothenberg. Abingdon, UK: Routledge.

Fryd, Vivien Green. 2001. *Art and Empire: The Politics of Ethnicity in the United States Capitol, 1815–1860*. Washington, DC: U.S. Capitol Historical Society. Distributed by Ohio University Press.

Garrett, Jeff, and Ron Guth. 2008. *Encyclopedia of U.S. Gold Coins, 1795–1933*. 3rd ed. Atlanta: Whitman Publishing.

Gilbert, Barbara Snow. 2007. "The Oklahoma Western District's Federal Courthouse." *Oklahoma Bar Review* 78 (2): 151–58.

Gilman, Carolyn. 2003. *Lewis and Clark: Across the Divide*. Washington, DC: Smithsonian Books.

Glassman, Matthew Eric. 2017. *U.S. Congressional Gold Medals, 1776–2014*. Congressional Research Service report. https://www.senate.gov/CRSpubs/d096b2b7-3221-4cec-b99c-3ba5774b0750.pdf.

Grafton, Anthony. (1992) 1995. *New World, Ancient Text: The Power of Tradition and the Shock of Discovery.* Cambridge, MA: Harvard University Press.

Greene, Candace. 2015. "Verbal Meets Visual: Sitting Bull and Representations of History." *Ethnohistory* 62 (2): 217–40.

Grossman, Lloyd. 2015. *Benjamin West and the Struggle to Be Modern*. London: Merrill Publishers.

Haley, J. C., E. Loran, and S. C. Pepper. 1964. *University of California: In Memoriam.* "John Ward Lockwood, Art: Berkeley, 1894–1963, Professor Emeritus." California Digital Library, University of California Libraries. Accessed July 29, 2016. http://texts.cdlib.org/view?docId=hb6g500784&doc.view=frames&chunk.id=div00008&toc.depth=1&toc.id=.

Hallowell, A. Irving, and Henry R. Schoolcraft. 1946. "Ojibwa Narratives in the Published Works of Henry R. Schoolcraft." *Journal of American Folklore* 59: 136–53.

Halsey, R. T. Haines, and Stanley Rolfe. 1939. *"Impolitical Prints": An Exhibition of Contemporary English Cartoons Relating to the American Revolution, Catalogue of the Exhibition.* New York Public Library.

Hamor, Ralph. (1615) 1957. *A True Discourse of the Present State of Virginia.* Richmond: Virginia State Library. https://archive.org/details/truediscourseofp1957hamo.

Hansen, Matthew. 2014. "New Mystery Arises from Iconic Iwo Jima Image." *Omaha World-Herald*, November 23.

Hastings, George E. 1926. *The Life and Work of Francis Hopkinson*. Chicago: University of Chicago Press.

Havard, Gilles. 2001. *The Great Peace of Montreal of 1701: French-Native Diplomacy in the Seventeenth Century*. Montreal: McGill-Queen's University Press.

Hebdige, Dick. 1979. *Subculture: The Meaning of Style*. London: Methuen.

Heckscher, William S. 1953. "Review of *Wild Men in the Middle Ages: A Study in Art, Sentiment, and Demonology.*" *Art Bulletin* 35 (3): 241–43.

Hinsley, Curtis M., Jr. 1981. *Savages and Scientists: The Smithsonian Institution and the Development of American Anthropology 1846–1910.* Washington, DC: Smithsonian Institution Press.

Hittman, Michael. 1996. "Wovoka (Jack Wilson)." In *Encyclopedia of North American Indians*, edited by Frederick E. Hoxie, 700–702. Boston: Houghton Mifflin.

Hixson, Walter L. 2013. *American Settler Colonialism: A History*. New York: Palgrave Macmillan.

Horsman, Reginald. 1999. "The Indian Policy of an 'Empire for Liberty.'" In *Native Americans and the Early Republic*, edited by Frederick E. Hoxie, Ronald Hoffman, and Peter J. Albert. Charlottesville: University Press of Virginia.

Hough, Walter. 1920. "Racial Groups and Figures in the Natural History Building of the United States National Museum." In *Annual Report Smithsonian Institution for Year Ending June 30, 1920.* Washington, DC: Smithsonian Institution.

Howe, Craig. 2006. "Feasting on Lewis and Clark." In *This Stretch of the River: Lakota, Dakota and Nakota Responses to the Lewis and Clark Expedition and Bicentennial,* edited by Craig Howe and Kim TallBear. Sioux Falls, SD: Pine Hill Press.

Howe, Craig and Kim TallBear. 2006. *This Stretch of the River: Lakota, Dakota and Nakota Responses to the Lewis and Clark Expedition and Bicentennial.* Sioux Falls, SD: Pine Hill Press.

Hoxie, Frederick E. 1996a. "Ghost Dance." In *Encyclopedia of North American Indians,* edited by Frederick E. Hoxie, 223. Boston: Houghton Mifflin.

———. 1996b. "Termination." In *Encyclopedia of North American Indians,* edited by Frederick E. Hoxie, 625. Boston: Houghton Mifflin.

———. 2001a. *A Final Promise: The Campaign to Assimilate the Indians, 1880–1920.* Lincoln: University of Nebraska Press.

———. 2001b. "Introduction: American Indian Activism in the Progressive Era." In *Talking Back to Civilization: Indian Voices from the Progressive Era,* edited by Frederick E. Hoxie, 1–28. Boston: Bedford/St. Martin's Press

———. 2007. "Introduction: What Can We Learn from a Bicentennial?" In *Lewis and Clark and the Indian Country,* edited by Frederick E. Hoxie and Jay T. Nelson, 1–16. Urbana and Chicago: University of Illinois Press.

———. 2012. *This Indian Country: American Indian Activists and the Place They Made.* New York: Penguin Press.

Huhndorf, Shari M. 2001. *Going Native: Indians in the American Cultural Imagination.* Ithaca, NY: Cornell University Press.

Hunt, Gaillard. 1909. *The History of the Seal of the United States.* Washington, DC: U.S. Department of State.

Impelluso, Lucia. (2003) 2004. *Nature and Its Symbols.* Translated by Stephen Sartarelli. Vol. 5 of *A Guide to Imagery.* Los Angeles: J. Paul Getty Museum.

Jackson, Donald D, ed. 1978. *Letters of the Lewis and Clark Expedition with Related Documents 1783–1854.* 2nd ed. Urbana: University of Illinois Press.

Jacobs, Margaret D. 2011. *White Mother to a Dark Race: Settler Colonialism, Maternalism, and the Removal of Indigenous Children in the American West and Australia, 1880–1940.* Lincoln: University of Nebraska Press.

Jacoby, Karl. 2008. *Shadow at Dawn: A Borderlands Massacre and the Violence of History.* New York: Penguin Press.

Johnson, Laura E. 2009. "'Goods to Clothe Themselves': Native Consumers and Native Images on the Pennsylvania Trading Frontier, 1712–1760." *Winterthur Portfolio* 43 (1): 115–40.

Johnson, Timothy. 2012. "Introduction." Speech given at "Richard Nixon and the American Indian: The Movement to Self-Determination," a symposium of the Smithsonian National Museum of the American Indian in collaboration with the National Archives and the Richard Nixon Foundation. Washington, DC, November 15. https://www.youtube.com/watch?v=jBUbD6Gb-BA.

Joyce, Dan. 1988. "Insignia of the Second Division, AEF." *Military Collector and Historian* 40 (2): 66–72.

Kappler, Charles J., ed. 1903. *Indian Affairs: Laws and Treaties,* vol. 2. Washington, DC: Government Printing Office.

Karshan, Donald H. 1968. "American Printmaking, 1670–1968." *Art in America* 56 (4): 22–55.

Kay, Rick. 2005. "The Remarkable Coinage of James B. Longacre." *The Numismatist* 118 (1-6): 36–37, 40–41.

Kennon, Donald R. and Thomas P. Somma, eds. 2004. *American Pantheon: Sculptural and Artistic Decoration of the United States Capitol.* Washington, DC: U.S. Capitol Historical Society. Distributed by Ohio University Press.

Kierner, Cynthia A. 2012. *Martha Jefferson Randolph, Daughter of Monticello: Her Life and Times.* Chapel Hill: University of North Carolina Press.

Kilroe, Edwin P. 1913. *Saint Tammany and the Origin of the Society of Tammany or Columbian Order in the City of New York.* New York: Columbia University Press.

King, Duane H., and Jefferson Chapman. 1993. *Official Guidebook to the Sequoyah Birthplace Museum.* Vonore, TN: Sequoyah Birthplace Museum.

Koeman, C. K. 1970. *Joan Blaeu and His Grand Atlas.* Amsterdam: Theatrum Orbis Terrarum.

Korshak, Yvonne. 1987. "The Liberty Cap as a Revolutionary Symbol in America and France." *Smithsonian Studies in American Art* 1 (2): 52–69.

Krogt, P. C. J. van der., ed. 2005. *Atlas Maior of 1665*. Köln, Germany: Taschen.

Lahontan, Louis Armand de Lom d'Arce, Baron de. (1703) 2012. *New Voyages to North America*, vol. 1. Providence, RI: John Carter Brown Library. https://archive.org/details/newvoyagestonort-03laho.

Lamar, Howard R. 1996. "Eastern Universities and Indians." In *Encyclopedia of North American Indians*, edited by Frederick E. Hoxie, 174–75. Boston: Houghton Mifflin.

Lange, David W. 1992. *The Complete Guide to Buffalo Nickels*. Virginia Beach, VA: DLRC Press.

Lawson, Michael L. 2009. *Dammed Indians Revisited: The Continuing History of the Pick-Sloan Plan and the Missouri River Sioux, 1944–1980*. Pierre: South Dakota State Historical Society Press.

Library of Congress. 2013. *Mapping a New Nation: Abel Buell's Map of the United States, 1784*. Washington, DC: Library of Congress. Exhibition brochure.

Lindsay, George W., Charles C. Conley, and Charles H. Litchman. (1893) 2015. *Official History of the Improved Order of Red Men: Compiled under Authority from the Great Council of the United States*. Boston: Fraternity Publishing Company.

Lockwood, J. Ward. 1940. "An Artist's Roots." *Magazine of Art* 33: 268–73.

Lupe, Ronnie. 1998. "Chairman's Vision: Message Given at Dedication Ceremonies for New Apache Longbow Helicopters." *Fort Apache Scout* 37 (13): 2.

———. 2013. "Chairman's Corner: The Veteran." *Fort Apache Scout* 52 (16): 3, 15.

Lurie, Nancy Oestreich. 1985. "Sacagawea." *North American Indian Lives*, edited by Nancy Oestreich Lurie, 31–35. Milwaukee, WI: Milwaukee Public Museum.

Lynn-Sherow, Bonnie. 1996. "Hayes, Ira." In *Encyclopedia of North American Indians*, edited by Frederick E. Hoxie, 236–37. Boston: Houghton Mifflin.

Mamdani, Mahmood. 2015. "Settler Colonialism: Then and Now." *Critical Inquiry* 41 (3): 596–614.

Marling, Karal Ann, and John Wetenhall. 1991. *Iwo Jima: Monuments, Memories, and the American Hero*. Cambridge, MA: Harvard University Press.

Maurer, Evan. 1984. "Dada and Surrealism." In *Primitivism in 20th Century Art*, vol. 2, edited by William Rubin, 535–594. New York: Museum of Modern Art.

McBeth, Sally. 1996. "Sacajawea." In *Encyclopedia of North American Indians*, edited by Frederick E. Hoxie, 562–63. New York: Houghton Mifflin.

McDermott, John D. 2010. *Red Cloud's War: The Bozeman Trail, 1866–1868*. Norman: University of Oklahoma Press.

McDonnell, Pete. 2009. "Integrity: A Lakota Value." Center for American Indian Research and Native Studies. http://www.nativecairns.org/CAIRNS/Lessons.html

McLerran, Jennifer. (2009) 2012. *A New Deal for Native Art: Indian Arts and Federal Policy 1933–1943*. Tucson: University of Arizona Press.

McMurtry, Larry. 2001. "Sacagawea's Nickname." *New York Review of Books*, September 20. http://www.nybooks.com/articles/2001/09/20/sacagaweas-nickname/.

McNally, Michael D. 2006. "The Indian Passion Play: Contesting the Real Indian in *Song of Hiawatha*, 1901–1905." *American Quarterly* 58 (1): 105–36.

McPherson, James. 2015. *Hallowed Ground: A Walk at Gettysburg*. Minneapolis: Zenith Press.

Meacham, Jon. 2013. *Thomas Jefferson: The Art of Power*. New York: Random House.

Medicine Crow, Joseph. 2003. *Counting Coup: Becoming a Crow Chief on the Reservation and Beyond*. Washington, DC: National Geographic Society.

Metropolitan Museum of Art. 2016. "Allegory of America." Accessed June 15. www.metmuseum.org/art/collection/search/335063.

Meyer, Roy. 1968. "Fort Berthold and the Garrison Dam." *North Dakota History: Journal of the Northern Plains* 35 (3, 4): 217–355.

Mick Gidley. 1998. *Edward S. Curtis and the North American Indian, Incorporated*. New York and Cambridge, UK: Cambridge University Press.

Miller Center for Public Affairs, University of Virginia. 2016. "Calvin Coolidge: Domestic Affairs." Accessed May 29. https://millercenter.org/president/coolidge/domestic-affairs.

Monkman, Betty C. 2000. *The White House: Its Historic Furnishings and First Families*. New York: Abbeville Press.

———. 2016. "The White House State Dinner." The White House Historical Association website. Accessed June 24. https://www.whitehousehistory.org/the-white-house-state-dinner.

Morehart, C. T. 2016. "Chinampa Agriculture, Surplus Production, and Political Change at Xaltocan, Mexico." *Ancient Mesoamerica* 27 (1): 183–96.

Morris, Edmund. 2001. *Theodore Rex.* New York: Random House.

Mott, Frank Luther. 1930. *A History of American Magazines: 1741–1850*, vol. 1. New York: D. Appleton.

Mt. Pleasant, Jane. 2006. "The Science Behind the Three Sisters Mound System." In *Histories of Maize: Multidisciplinary Approaches to Prehistory, Linguistics, Biogeography, Domestication, and Evolution of Maize*, edited by John Staller, Robert Tykot, and Bruce Benz, 529–38. New York: Academic Press.

Mushkat, Jerome. 1971. *Tammany: The Evolution of a Political Machine, 1789–1865*. Syracuse, NY: Syracuse University Press.

Nalty, Bernard C., and Danny J. Crawford. 1995. *The United States Marines on Iwo Jima: The Battle and the Flag Raisings*. Washington, DC: History and Museums Division, U.S. Marine Corps. http://www.teachwithmovies.org/guides/flags-of-our-fathers-files/The%20United%20States%20 Marines%20On%20Iwo%20Jima_The%20 Battle%20and%20the%20Flag%20Raisings%20 %20PCN%2019000316600.pdf.

National Research Council. 2014. *Review of Department of Defense Test Protocols for Combat Helmets*. Washington, DC: National Academies Press.

Nelson, Dale W. 2003. *Interpreters with Lewis and Clark: The Story of Sacagawea and Toussaint Charbonneau*. Denton: University of North Texas Press.

New York Times. 1871a. "An Indian Massacre." May 31, 5.

New York Times. 1871b. "The Camp Grant Massacre." July 29, 1.

New York Times. 1891. "Its Monument Dedicated; The Tammany Regiment on the Gettysburg Field. Gen. Sickles and Other Orators Tell of the Brave Deeds of Its Members Which the Handsome Monument Is to Commemorate." September 25, 2.

New York Times. 1905. "Roosevelt Hero of a Brilliant Day." March 5, 1.

New York Times. 1912. "Athlete Thorpe to Quit Indian School." November 26, 13.

New York Times. 1913. "Sioux Chief Hollow Horn Bear Dead." March 16, 8.

New York Times. 1927a. "May Make Coolidge Sioux, Indians of the Black Hills Talk of Adopting President." June 12, 19.

New York Times. 1927b. "Coolidge to Be 'Leading Eagle.'" July 31, 159.

New York Times. 1927c. "Coolidge Becomes Chief of Sioux." August 5, 1, 3.

New York Times. 1933a. "Roosevelt Tells Boy Scouts of NRA." August 24, 17.

New York Times. 1933b. "Text of Address by President Roosevelt Before 1,000 Boy Scouts at Encampment." August 24, 17.

New York Times. 1950. "Jim Thorpe Named Greatest in Sport." February 12, 142.

New York Times. 1952. "Indians Lose Land in Path of Big Dam." June 11, 27.

New York Times. 1953a. "Jim Thorpe Is Dead on West Coast at 64." March 29, 1, 92.

New York Times. 1953b. "The End of the Trail." October 13, 28.

New York Times. 1954. "Topic of the Times." November 9, 26.

Newhall, Beaumont. (1982) 2009. *The History of Photography from 1839 to the Present*. New York: Museum of Modern Art.

Office of U.S. Marine Corps Communication. 2016. "USMC Statement on Iwo Jima Flag Raisers." Posted June 23. http://www.marines. mil/News/News-Display/Article/810457/usmc-statement-on-iwo-jima-flagraisers/.

Olson, Lester C. 1991. "The Colonies Are an Indian." In *Emblems of American Community in the Revolutionary Era: A Study in Rhetorical Iconography*, vol. 1. Washington, DC: Smithsonian Institution Press.

Order Sons of Italy in America. 2003. "Honoring Diversity: A Selection of Commemorative U.S. Postage Stamps." http://www.osia.org/documents/ Stamp.pdf.

Parker, James. 1929. "The Geronimo Campaign." *Proceedings of the Annual Meeting and Dinner of the Order of Indian Wars of the United States*. Washington, DC: Army and Navy Club.

Patterson, Richard S., and Richardson Dougall. 1976. *The Eagle and the Shield: A History of the Great Seal of the United States*. Washington DC: U.S. Department of State.

Pearce, Roy Harvey. (1953) 1967. *Savagism and Civilization: A Study of the Indian and the American Mind*. Baltimore: Johns Hopkins University Press.

Peck, Amelia. 2013. "'India Chints' and 'China Taffaty': East India Textiles for the North American Market." In *Interwoven Globe: The Worldwide Textile Trade, 1500–1800*, edited by Amelia Peck, 104–19. New York: Metropolitan Museum of Art.

Pitcher, Edward W. R. 2001. *The Royal American Magazine, 1774–1775: An Annotated Catalogue*. Lewiston, NY: E. Mellon Press.

Rauner Library. 2011. "What's with the Arrow in His Head?" http://raunerlibrary.blogspot.com/2011/08/whats-with-arrow-in-his-head.html.

Reynolds, Clifford P. 1961. *Biographical Directory of the American Congress, 1774–1961: The Continental Congress, September 5, 1774, to October 21, 1788 and the Congress of the United States, from the First to the Eighty-sixth Congress, March 4, 1789, to January 3, 1961, Inclusive*. Washington, DC: U.S. Government Printing Office.

Reynolds, Donald Martin. 1993. *Masters of American Sculpture: The Figurative Tradition from the American Renaissance to the Millennium*. New York: Abbeville Press.

Ronda, James P. 1984. *Lewis and Clark among the Indians*. Lincoln: University of Nebraska Press.

Rountree, Helen C., and E. Randolph Turner III. (2002) 2005. *Before and After Jamestown: Virginia's Powhatans and Their Predecessors*. Gainesville: University of Florida Press.

Rowe, John Howland. 1965. "The Renaissance Foundations of Anthropology." *American Anthropologist* 67 (1): 1–20.

Salmon, Emily Jones, and John Salmon. 2013. "Tobacco in Colonial Virginia." In *Encyclopedia Virginia*. Charlottesville: Virginia Foundation for the Humanities. http://www.EncyclopediaVirginia.org/Tobacco_in_Colonial_Virginia.

Scanlon, Donna. 2009. "The Bronze Doors of the Library of Congress." *Inside Adams* (blog). Library of Congress. https://blogs.loc.gov/inside_adams/2009/12/our-bronze-doors/.

Scigliano, Robert, ed. 2001. *The Federalist: A Commentary on the Constitution of the United States*. New York: Modern Library.

Sickles, Daniel E. 2004. "Dedication of Monument, 42d Regiment Infantry, September 24, 1891, Oration." New York State Division of Military and Naval Affairs. https://dmna.ny.gov/historic/reghist/civil/infantry/42ndInf/42ndInfHistSketch.htm.

Siegriest, Louis. 1975. Oral history interview conducted by Paul Karlstrom and Nathan Oliveira, for the Archives of American Art, Smithsonian Institution. April 5. http://www.aaa.si.edu/collections/interviews/oral-history-interview-louis-siegriest-13217.

Skemp, Sheila L. 1999. "Paul Revere: Artisan Republican." *Reviews in American History* 27 (4): 368–72. doi: 10.1353/rah.1999.0064.

Smith, John. (1624) 2006. *The Generall Historie of Virginia, New England & the Summer Isles. . .* Chapel Hill: University Library, UNC-Chapel Hill and University of North Carolina at Chapel Hill. http://docsouth.unc.edu/southlit/smith/smith.html.

Smith, Paul Chaat. 2009. *Everything You Know about Indians Is Wrong*. Minneapolis: University of Minnesota Press.

Smith, Sherry L. 2000. *Reimagining Indians: Native Americans through Anglo Eyes, 1880–1940*. New York: Oxford University Press.

Smithers, Gregory D. 2014. *Native Diasporas: Indigenous Identities and Settler Colonialism in the Americas*. Lincoln: University of Nebraska Press.

Sonneborn, Liz. (1998) 2007. "Thorpe, Grace." In *A to Z of American Indian Women, Revised Edition*. New York: Infobase Publishing.

Speck, Frank Gouldsmith. 1925. "The Penn Wampum Belts." *Leaflets of the Museum of the American Indian, Heye Foundation*, no. 4. New York: Museum of the American Indian, Heye Foundation.

Stevens, Henry, and Roland Tree. 1951. *Comparative Cartography Exemplified in an Analytical & Bibliographical Description of Nearly One Hundred Maps and Charts of the American Continent Published in Great Britain During the Years 1600 to 1850*. Urbana: University of Illinois Urbana-Champaign. https://archive.org/details/comparativecarto00stev.

Stokes, I. N. Phelps. 1915. *The Iconography of Manhattan Island, 1498–1909*, vol. 1. New York: Robert H. Dodd.

Storing, Herbert J. 1981. *What the Anti-Federalists Were For: The Political Thought of the Opponents of the Constitution*. Chicago: University of Chicago Press.

Sturtevant, William. 1976. "First Visual Images of Native America." In *First Images of America: The Impact of the New World on the Old*, edited by Fredi Chiappelli, Michael J. B. Allen, and Robert L. Benson. Berkeley: University of California Press.

Sweeney, Edwin R. 1997. *Making Peace with Cochise: The 1872 Journal of Captain Joseph Alton Sladen*. Norman: University of Oklahoma Press.

———. 2010. *From Cochise to Geronimo: The Chiricahua Apaches, 1874–1886*. Norman: University of Oklahoma Press.

Taxay, Don. 1966. *The U.S. Mint and Coinage*. New York: Arco Publishing.

Thenault, George. 1921. *The Story of the Lafayette Escadrille*. Translated by Walter Duranty. Boston: Small, Maynard & Company.

Thorpe, Grace F. 1981. "The Jim Thorpe Family: From Wisconsin to Indian Territory." *Chronicles of Oklahoma* 59 (1): 91–105 and 59 (2): 179–201.

Thorpe, Grace. 1996. "Jim Thorpe (1887–1953) Sauk and Fox Football and Baseball Player and Olympic Athlete." In *Encyclopedia of North American Indians*, edited by Frederick E. Hoxie. New York: Houghton Mifflin.

Trachtenberg, Alan. 2004. *Shades of Hiawatha: Staging Indians, Making Americans, 1880–1930*. New York: Hill and Wang.

Tyson, Job R. 1836. *Discourse on the Surviving Remnant of the Indian Race in the United States*. Washington, DC: Library of Congress. https://archive.org/details/discourseonsurvi00tyso.

U.S. Army Publishing Directorate. 2014. *Army Acquisition Procedures*. Department of the Army Pamphlet 70-3. March 11. http://www.apd.army.mil/epubs/DR_pubs/DR_a/pdf/web/p70_3.pdf.

U.S. Department of the Interior. 2016. "Interior Museum Online Murals Tour." Accessed May 14. https://www.doi.gov/interiormuseum/Tours.

U.S. Department of State, Bureau of Public Affairs. 2003. *The Great Seal of the United States*. https://www.state.gov/documents/organization/27807.pdf.

U.S. Department of State, Office of the Historian. 2016. "1784–1800: The Diplomacy of the Early Republic." Accessed May 16. https://history.state.gov/milestones/1784-1800/foreword.

U.S. Department of Veterans Affairs. 2012. *American Indian and Alaska Native Servicemembers and Veterans*. https://www.va.gov/TRIBALGOVERNMENT/docs/AIAN_Report_FINAL_v2_7.pdf.

U.S. Mint. 2016a. "Code Talkers Recognition Congressional Medals Program." Last modified November 10. https://www.usmint.gov/learn/coin-and-medal-programs/medals/native-american-code-talkers.

U.S. Mint. 2016b. "Sacagawea Golden Dollar Coin." Last reviewed June 1. https://www.usmint.gov/coins/coin-medal-programs/sacagawea-golden-dollar.

University of Pennsylvania. 2016. "Penn Biographies: Francis Hopkinson (1737–1791)." University of Pennsylvania Archives and Records Center. Accessed May 18. http://www.archives.upenn.edu/people/1700s/hopkinson_fra.html.

Viola, Herman J. 1981. *Diplomats in Buckskins: A History of Indian Delegations in Washington D.C.* Washington, DC: Smithsonian Institution Press.

Voltaire. (1733) 2007. *Philosophical Letters: Or, Letters Regarding the English Nation*, edited by John Leigh. Translated by Prudence L. Steiner. Indianapolis: Hackett Publishing Company.

Washburn, Wilcomb E., ed. 1988. *History of Indian-White Relations*. Vol 4 of *Handbook of North American Indians*, edited by William C. Sturtevant. Washington, DC: Smithsonian Institution.

West, Chris. 2014. *A History of America in Thirty-six Postage Stamps*. New York: Picador.

Wheeler, Robert W. 1979. *Jim Thorpe: World's Greatest Athlete*. Norman: University of Oklahoma Press.

Whitcomb, Peter. 2015. "Information on Soils and Soil Health: The Three Sisters." U.S. Department of Agriculture Natural Resources Conservation Service. https://content.govdelivery.com/accounts/USDANRCS/bulletins/12897b3.

Whitehill, Walter Muir, and Sinclair H. Hitchings, eds. 1973. *Boston Prints and Printmakers, 1670–1775: A Conference Held by the Colonial Society of Massachusetts, 1 and 2 April 1971*. Charlottesville: University Press of Virginia.

Wolfe, Brendan. 2015. "Colonial Virginia." In *Encyclopedia Virginia*. Charlottesville: Virginia Foundation for the Humanities. http://www.EncyclopediaVirginia.org/Colonial_Virginia.

Wolfe, Patrick. 2006. "Settler Colonialism and the Elimination of the Native." *Journal of Genocide Research* 8 (4): 387–409.

Woodson, M. Kyle. 2015. "Hohokam Canal Irrigation and the Formation of Irragric Anthrosols in the Middle Gila River Valley, Arizona, USA." *Geoarchaeology*, 30 (4): 271–90.

Acknowledgments

The idea for this book grew out of curatorial discussions that took place during the development of the National Museum of the American Indian (NMAI) exhibition *Americans*, specifically its introductory section titled "Indians Everywhere." Conceived by the exhibition's lead curator, Paul Chaat Smith, this section explores the pervasiveness of American Indian imagery in Americans' everyday lives—as evidence of Americans' and American Indians' deeply entangled history. In the course of our discussions, it became clear that the role of the U.S. government in the production of this imagery merited closer examination. I begin therefore by thanking Paul for the opportunity to collaborate with him in creating the exhibition, and for his support for this book. I thank the NMAI Publications Assessment Group and publications manager Tanya Thrasher for their belief in the book as well. Thanks to Tanya, as well, for her negotiations with the book's distributor, the University of Minnesota Press, and to Jason Weidemann, the press's editorial director, for his commitment to the book. *Officially Indian* would not have been possible without the full support of NMAI director Kevin Gover, associate director David W. Penney, supervisory curator Ann McMullen, and project manager Travis Helms. To them, I am most grateful.

I express my deepest gratitude to Colin G. Calloway, professor of history and Native American studies at Dartmouth College, and to Paul Chaat Smith, respectively, for their foreword and afterword. Their essays add considerable dimension. Among the many people I want to thank for helping me identify emblems, or for sharing their expertise about the emblems' details or historical context are: Tony Abeyta, Diné artist; Bruce Bernstein, the executive director of the Continuous Pathways Foundation; Owen Linlithgow Conner, the curator of uniforms and heraldry at the National Museum of the Marine Corps; Oliver Enjady, Mescalero Apache artist; Carolyn Gilman, a historian and senior exhibition developer at the NMAI;

Duane Hollow Horn Bear, a Lakota tribal historian; David R. Hunt, an anthropologist at the National Museum of Natural History; Ira Jacknis, the head of research and publications at the Phoebe A. Hearst Museum of Anthropology; Amelia Brakeman Kile, a museum specialist at the National Air and Space Museum; Duane H. King, the director of the Helmerich Center for American Research; John McClure, the director of Research Services at the Virginia Historical Society; Christopher Moore, a museum specialist at the National Air and Space Museum; Felicia Pickering, an ethnology collections specialist at the National Museum of Natural History; Jen Shannon, an associate professor and curator at the University of Colorado, Boulder; Alex M. Spencer, a curator at the National Air and Space Museum; Herman Viola, curator emeritus at the National Museum of Natural History; Greg Weinman, senior legal counsel at the United States Mint; Leslie Wheelock, the director of the Office of Tribal Relations at the United States Department of Agriculture; and M. Kyle Woodson of the Cultural Resource Management Program at the Gila River Community. I also owe my thanks to Elayne Silversmith, the librarian at the National Museum of the American Indian's Vine Deloria Jr. Library.

I must express my sincere thanks to the two anonymous reviewers who carefully read an earlier version of manuscript. Their thoughtful critiques yielded a stronger final draft. Along those lines, I need to thank Paul Chaat Smith and NMAI editor Sally Barrows for their substantive editorial suggestions. Both helped me clarify and sharpen my text. Sally Barrows was instrumental in overseeing all editorial phases of *Officially Indian*. NMAI editor Alexandra Harris Schupman helped shoulder editorial work at a crucial juncture. Both are owed a special debt of gratitude.

Special thanks to Susan Pourian, the director of the Indian Craft Shop at the U.S. Department of the Interior, for her gracious assistance in providing access to the Allan Houser mural *Breaking Camp during Wartime* and to photographer Alex Jamison for his digital image of the mural. I also thank Leslie K. Overstreet, the curator of natural-history rare books at the Smithsonian's Joseph F. Cullman 3rd Library of Natural History for kindly providing us with a digital image of the cover of volume 3 of Henry Rowe Schoolcraft's *Historical and Statistical Information Respecting the History, Condition, and Prospects of the Indian Tribes of the United States*.

Finally, I am indebted to NMAI curatorial project assistant Julie B. Macander for securing all other digital images and credits published in this book, and to Wendy Hurlock Baker, NMAI's rights and reproductions manager, for securing permissions needed to reproduce the images. And I express my heartfelt gratitude to NMAI designer Steve Bell for the book's handsome cover and layout.

—Cécile R. Ganteaume

Index

184